*English Literature in our Time
and the University*

ENGLISH LITERATURE
IN OUR TIME
& THE UNIVERSITY

THE CLARK LECTURES
1967

F. R. Leavis

1969

CHATTO & WINDUS

LONDON

Published by
Chatto & Windus Ltd
40 William IV Street
London W.C.2

*

Clarke, Irwin & Co. Ltd
Toronto

SBN 7011 1517 3

Printed in Great Britain by
T. & A. Constable Ltd., Edinburgh

To the Memory of
H. MUNRO CHADWICK & MANSFIELD D. FORBES
to whom the world owes more than it knows

Acknowledgments

The quotations from *Collected Poems 1909-1962* by T. S. Eliot appear by permission of Faber & Faber Ltd., London, and Harcourt, Brace and World Inc., New York. *Copyright* © 1936 by Harcourt, Brace and World Inc. and *Copyright* © 1963, 1964 by T. S. Eliot.

Contents

INTRODUCTORY

I HAVE ceased trying to devise a better title for this book than that under which I delivered its contents as Clark lecturer at Cambridge in the Lent Term 1967: it has come to seem to me as good a title as any that could be found. The precise intended force is something that had to be defined by the book itself; but that must have been so with any title and I might properly, perhaps, at the cost of seeming grandiloquent, have said that it has to be created, so strong is my sense of the difficulty of getting the nature of my theme and preoccupation recognized. The paired terms—the associated ideas or significances, 'English literature' and 'the University', as I am concerned with them—ought not, I feel, to meet with the unreadiness for intelligent recognition and response that in fact they do. That way of putting it expresses my sense of the urgent gravity of what is at issue, a frightening face of the gravity being the blankness—the inability, or refusal, to perceive—that characterizes our civilization.

My title won't at worst give rise to expectations as wide of the mark as those incurred by Ruskin when he called one of his works *Notes on the Construction of Sheepfolds*. And I will immediately, anticipating the text that follows, disclaim two promises that might be read into the title. I am not, then, offering anything in the nature of a survey, critical and descriptive, of what has been written in our time, and I am not proposing a syllabus for an ideal English course at the University.

What I am concerned with is the way in which 'English literature' exists at any time as a living reality, and the need, which imposes convinced and resourceful effort of a kind I make it my aim to define, that it should exist as such for us—that it should be in civilization a real and potent force in our time. This last phrase is an insistence on the fact of change. Life is growth and change in response to changing conditions, and modern civilization advances in the spirit of its triumphant logic at such a rate that the fact of change is taken for granted. It is taken for granted in such a way that the profounder human consequences and significances of unceasing rapid and accelerating change escape notice. The deduction I draw is that our time faces us with a new necessity of conscious provision: we have to make provision for keeping alive, potent and developing that full human consciousness of ends and values and human nature that comes to us (or should) out of the long creative continuity of our culture. And this brings me to 'the University'.

I won't offer to summarize the evocation of 'university' I attempt in the following book; I will merely, for my prefatory purpose, recall some main emphases. The first must be that the 'university' is the inevitable, the inescapable, answer to the question: What would provision of the kind needed be like? There is no other that could be seriously proposed. It follows at once from this considered and wholly confident assertion of mine that neither the College of Technology exalted (to Mr Harold Wilson's satisfaction)[1] into a degree-conferring university, nor the Open University promised us, is a university in what it is my business to insist on as the important sense.

[1] As at once a blow to snobbery and a means of advancing the desired multiplication.

2

The real university is a centre of consciousness and human responsibility for the civilized world; it is a creative centre of civilization—for the living heritage on which meaning and humane intelligence depend can't, in our time, be maintained without a concentrated creativity somewhere.

It should be plain that my concern for 'English literature' implies no slighting of the sciences, or the other specialist studies. On the contrary, I postulate the co-presence of the specialist studies in general, representing unequivocally high standards, with a strong humane centre, and this I give my reasons for seeing as an English School. The problem is to *have* an English School that truly deserves the respect of those who are acquainted with intellectual standards in their own fields—for only such can do anything to make a constituted university more than the mere collocation of specialist departments it tends to be. The difficulty of achieving and maintaining serious standards in the field of literary study is that that field, in the nature of its distinctive discipline of intelligence, is at the other extreme from mathematics—to say which is to point to the nature of its importance. The modes of thought distinctive of the field entail, as essential to—as essentially in and of—the thinking, kinds of judgment of quality and value that don't admit of demonstrative enforcement. About the relevant standards, how they are generated and what their authority is, I have tried to speak with clarity and the requisite fulness in my first lecture. Here I will only point to certain conditions that impose themselves where it is a question of realizing the idea of the university: the students in English too must be of university quality, capable of a high level of work and with a genuine and intelligent interest in literature, and secondly, the permanent school must be staffed with seniors qualified to take pleasure in 'teaching' such pupils—that is, to find working with them a profitable kind of collaboration.

This last term has a pregnant centrality to my theme, as my lectures will bring out. Here, in these prefatory reflections, it leads me to certain emphases in relation to doubts and questions I am aware of. I have spoken of the 'monstrous unrealism' of the expectation commonly entertained of the undergraduates; but can they, it will be asked, reasonably be supposed capable of meeting the demand I myself make of them? My answer is that, provided the conditions I lay down are observed, most certainly they can: doubters are suspect of ignoring the conditions and misconceiving the nature of the demand —and my actual demand is in implication an account of what a university should be. I sometimes wonder what answer the comfortably institutional academic in English arrives at when he asks himself (if he does) what, in terms of any serious idea of a university education, he positively counts on the undergraduates' being able to do and acquire. My own answer to such a challenge I have, in my lectures, indicated in the way determined by the complex and difficult undertaking to which I was committed. With that careful presentation to point to, I will offer nothing more here than a few tactical emphases, or re-emphases, addressed to doubters or those who have to deal with them.

What, then, worth doing does one assume that undergraduates will be able to do? One assumes—from experience one knows—that, with the help they ought to be able to get from maturer students in the school (and surely some of their appointed guides should genuinely and happily be describable as that), they will learn what reading is and what thinking is—those intimately associated capacities. By 'reading' and 'thinking' I mean the kinds characterizing the discipline of intelligence that belongs to the field of literary criticism (and that there is such a discipline, the importance of which to civilization needs with peculiar urgency to be vindicated in our time, is what I aim at making plain in my extended argument). A student may be said to have got his initiation into 'reading' and 'thinking' by the time he has come to intelligent critical terms with, and made himself, with personal conviction, intelligently articulate about, two or three of the great Shakespeare plays, two or three major novels, and some poems of diverse kind by great poets. By putting it in this way I mean to suggest how early in his course the student can and should, feel himself started—confident of help and stimulus, but self-reliant—on a development of powers and interests and understanding that *is* education as 'university' promises it.

Of course, to have done the things I have suggested he would have done a good deal more than just that—more, that is, than such a list of things 'done' seems to cover. If you do a critique of *Little Dorrit*, that book won't be all of Dickens you've read, and the doing will inevitably lead to further reading and thinking. And if you know Dickens, you won't be content with knowing Dickens alone. And Dickens leads you into the study of Victorian civilization, leading you on at the same time into extended, and still further extended, acquaintance with the novelists.

In the sense it is my business to insist on (it is the sense in which the words and the phrase need to be

ENGLISH LITERATURE IN OUR TIME

used in relation to a university English School and the discipline of intelligence on which the claim of English to respect depends) to 'learn to read and to think' is to be launched on the acquiring of a distinctive grasp of history. I aimed in my Clark lectures at demonstrating what I meant by saying that. It was a difficult undertaking, exposed, I'm afraid, in spite of a precautionary preface and a reminder from time to time, to being wrongly taken. Here I will only repeat that what I offered I offered as suggestive illustration, chosen and developed so as to define the nature of my intention and convey in concrete terms the force of my argument and plea. I thought (and think) the judgments entailed in my historical draft-notes sound enough, but I did my best to ensure that no one should forget the 'this is so, isn't it?' of the spirit in which I advanced them. I needed to keep constantly present to my audience, for recognition and intelligent appreciation, the conditions of collaborative interplay in which (a basic assumption) I assume the students' reading and thinking to be carried on.

And this brings me to the head of 'incompleteness'. In relation to the problem, or complex of problems, I am considering, the idea of completeness (except as necessarily implicit in the recognition of inevitable incompleteness) has no useful function. I can refer forward here with immediate and obvious point to my comments on the once familiar case for making the Classics— Greek and Latin literature—the staple of humane education:[1] 'the literatures are complete; all the rules are known.' That states classically an attitude and a set of preconceptions that make any real recognition of the

[1] See page 68 below.

6

problem facing—or engulfing—us impossible. English literature—it is that, not arbitrarily but with a quintessential relevance, we are concerned with as we consider the state and prospects of our civilization—has its reality and life (if at all) only in the present. The problem is to maintain the full vital continuity of our culture. I won't try to summarize here what I shall be found to say in my lectures about the necessity, in relation to that problem, of there being a strong informing presence of the 'reality and life'—of the life as a potent reality that transcends the present—in the rapidly changing civilization of our time.

Pressed as to the nature of such a presence, one can only reply that it has to be created; it is created by the kind of implicit collaboration that creates and maintains a language. But the collaborators are individuals who are interested in literature, convinced that it matters, and intelligent about it, and the collaboration is an interplay of personal judgments. Where the interest is widely enough spread, the outcome of the interplay will be something approaching a consensus as to what English Literature, the truly living reality, is—for us. I might have added 'or ought to be'; but the distinction in this matter between ideal felt with conviction to be valid and fact or reality is a tricky one. The 'for us' is of course a crucial emphasis. Here it leads immediately to the observation that 'we' shall not be naïve enough to suppose ourselves representative in any final way. As the inner sense of stress, tension and human need changes, English Literature changes—not merely (I mean) by accretion; the contour map, the chart of organic structure, changes. Without the genuine creative response there is no reality of art. But the collaborative creativity of the cultivated public is not, for being creative, to be thought of as arbitrary: it is (so long as there is recognition) the only genuine mode of recognizing something that is 'there'— a mode that entails constant revision. There is no contradiction between saying these things and perceiving that English Literature must be different for every age.

To talk of 'completeness', then, would be to use a term that implied an irrelevant ethos and a misleading emphasis and inflexion. What matters for each age is coherence—significant relatedness in an organic whole, the centre of significance being (inevitably) the present. With these considerations in mind I come back to the situation of the undergraduate. At any point in his student career his 'English Literature' will be patchy and partial, but, properly guided, he will in acquiring his knowledge of his selected areas and themes be forming a sense of the whole to which they belong and which they implicitly postulate. And here comes another consideration, of a different order from the last but intimately associated with it: he will at the same time be developing a strong sense of himself 'belonging' as he reads and thinks and works at organizing his knowledge and thought; and this sense —one of belonging to a collaborative community, the essential nucleus of which is the permanent English School—will play a very important part in the force and effectiveness with which he realizes the fact, and the nature of the existence, of 'English Literature'.

Of course, I assume an English School of which the permanent or senior members are qualified in the ways I posited as obviously proper for those who hold such posts. And if the School were the liaison centre it might be and (I have contended) ought to be, the student in belonging to it would belong—his work would make him actively aware he belonged—to a wider, a more comprehensive, community of intellectual collaboration in which the idea of the university was realized; the idea of it, I mean, as a creative centre, for the civilized world, of real human responsibility. I am not supposing that the idea would be there, consciously entertained and active, in any but a small proportion of the total academic personnel; but in relation to the kind of issue in question quantitative measures can say little to the point. What matters is to have a strong centre of life; its power to inform, animate and impart vital significance may be immensely disproportionate to its statistical magnitude.

In belonging to such a centre the undergraduate will have a direct quintessential acquaintance with the self-perpetuation (necessarily recreative) of a living culture. The 'direct' insists that this is not the plane of theory; acquaintance is participation, active and conscious, in the one culture of which this could be so—his own. In working out what can be done in his three years he is collaborating with his guides and advisers and fellow-students—with, in sum, the total continuous life of the centre—to determine what in our time English Literature, the living reality, is, or ought to be. The collaborative community gives him, he can tell himself, the focused presence of that potentially decisive educated public to foster which, strengthening it, giving it an informed awareness of its rôle in the face of the euphoric regardlessness of technological progress, and qualifying it for the influence desperate human need calls on it to exert, is the constitutive function of the university.

I know the comment that will come and with what dismissing inflection: 'you talk as if such a state of things

in a university were possible—and you denounce academic
unrealism!' But why, I ask, have we to judge it impossible, and in what sense? I should never suggest that
the achieving would be easy, having strong reason for
being realistic about what lies in the way. There is a
familiar trait of human nature that, being in English
Schools unchecked by the authority of clear, relevant and
unquestionable criteria, can determine the recruitment
of staff. Where the staff doesn't comprise from the outset, if not a majority, at least a strong nucleus of members
who are intelligent about literature and charged with disinterested concern for their function it will hardly tend
by recruitment to make itself different, except for the
worse. And, for anyone who, sharing my kind of solicitude, looks round at the academic scene, this is un-
deniably a discouraging consideration.

But it is not a consideration one stops at; it is a way of
recognizing the necessity, in our civilization, of a strongly
positive conception of the university and the English
School. If anyone feels that 'conception' here sounds
weak, he should remind himself that to conceive what is
needed entails impulsion and purpose; the conception,
embodying a realization of the human plight in our time,
a matter of innermost human nature starved and thwarted,
is the profoundest kind of creative response. It will
certainly be active, initiating and pertinacious only in a
small minority, but it may transform civilization—this
more than merely intellectual conviction is of the essence
of it.

I didn't say 'a *new* conception'; that would have been
to slight the strength that resides in continuity. The
newness is a matter of development, and of formulation
in terms of the present world and the way it is now so

unmistakably going. But there *is* the strength; the conception has its past, awareness of which can only intensify one's sense of the validity, the historical significance and the realism.

Possibly most of those concerned about the issues know that the foundation at Cambridge towards the close of the first world war of the English Tripos was an important event in history. Nevertheless the contemptuous resistance offered to the idea of making, at an ancient English university, the critical study of English Literature the rival of Classics as 'humane education' is becoming difficult to recall. On the other hand, in referring to the 'idea' in this way I shall have conveyed a false impression unless I go on to say that my formulation would hardly have occurred to a majority of the main promoters of the new Tripos as describing what they planned to do. For one thing, what the 'critical study of English literature' might be—could or should be—had yet to be worked out; the working out was one of the consequences of starting the English Tripos.

Looking back, no one can seriously deny that the new Tripos was a creative response to change—change in society and civilization that had been made unignorable by the war. But to one looking back, inquiringly, in the nineteen-twenties it could seem to be very much the product of some happy accidents that had converged to this one end. To begin with, there the fact that Oxford had got in first in the recognition of the native tongue, and, in making it possible to read for Honours in English, had (inevitably, before the revolutionary consequences of the Cambridge innovation) imposed on the student the academic ethos that expresses itself in compulsory Anglo-Saxon and the naïve associated notions of 'language' and 'discipline'. Cambridge, late enough in the field to find its prompting in the prospective needs of after-the-war, arrived at the obvious decision to be initiatory, leave Oxford in the nineteenth century with London, and strike boldly out with the institution of a distinctly literary English course.

The occupant of the lonely and despised already existing Chair of English Literature, Q, was no Anglo-Saxonist, but even if the cause of literature had been represented by a stronger positive idea than his of what intelligent literary study at the university and a central humane school might be, clear reason alone could not have inflicted on the entrenched and determined enemy the crushing defeat actually suffered—and never forgiven: the refusal to make Anglo-Saxon compulsory. The decisive fact was another accident: Cambridge was not without its Chair of Anglo-Saxon, and the Professor was a man of great distinction, rare disinterestedness and clear views, and uncompromising resolution. What the student reading English at Cambridge during the past half century, and what the cause in general for which I am concerned, owes to Hector Munro Chadwick will be found set forth by a pupil of his in *Scrutiny* (Volume XIV, 3).[1] I need record here only this much: he contended that the study of Anglo-Saxon went properly, not with the study of English Literature, but with the study of the whole culture-complex of the North, and he testified that only a few students—he himself wanted only such —could be interested enough to profit by the attempt to learn Anglo-Saxon. Compulsory Anglo-Saxon, he said, was wasteful (and worse) not only for the student of

[1] Reprinted in *A Selection from Scrutiny*, Volume I, page 41. (Cambridge University Press).

literature, but also for the scholar who, knowing why he himself is serious about Anglo-Saxon, has to try and teach it to the uninterested.

Q, who felt that he believed in literature, and that literature should both impart taste and be kept in touch with life, rejoiced at the defeat of the Anglo-Saxonists. His own taste was a very conventional product of the civilization that had formed him in his late-Victorian Oxford days, though, being himself manly, he was unconscious of the aesthetic affiliation of his ideal, a stylistic one, of good writing. His conception of the new school was that, making Aristotle's Poetics (in Butcher's or Bywater's translation) the handbook of critical thought, it should inculcate (and reward) good taste, good writing and decent manliness. The worst to be said about it is not that it gave no hint of any exploratory-creative energy that would be needed to justify the innovation and realize the implicit promise of the charter, but that it represented the most dangerous enemy that threatened the English Tripos in its first decade. This was the supremely confident 'Classical' tradition of Form, Latin-versifier's taste, conventional externality and belles-lettres. A large proportion of those teaching, lecturing and examining for the Tripos were products of Classics— some of them just lending a hand with English by the way, while regarding the Classical Tripos as their serious business. Indeed, it was offensive in those days to question the belief (shared by Q) that to have taken the Classical Tripos with credit qualified you to teach for the English. How real the menace was—or had been— may be deduced from the fact that at the very close of the decade Bridges' *The Testament of Beauty* (pedestrian audacities of 'technique' applied to jejune disquisitory prosings) and Meredith's *Modern Love* were prescribed as texts for special study.

My parenthetic 'or had been' registers my recollection of the tacit defeat that ensued: no such demonstration—it was assertively deliberate—occurred again. The finality of the episode gives its significance: it was too late; the distinctive tradition of Cambridge English had by then been generated and had developed its own robust life. This was not a result of any institutional lead; it expressed no institutional intention. What the happy immunity together with the scheme of studies authorized by the framers of the Tripos had done was to make the intelligent study of literature possible: they had provided the opportunity.

It was Mansfield Forbes who, from the very outset, ensured that the opportunity should be taken. Accident determined that, at the moment when his gifts of character and intelligence could tell decisively, he was at hand: the circumstances of war-time Cambridge gave him an unforeseeable chance—thrust it upon him. Young, convinced, contagiously charged with energy and irrepressible, he performed during those opening years of Cambridge English—the dark late years of the war—the service he was unmistakably and irrepressibly fitted for. There was the charter, there was an examination to be held under it in two years time, there was no Faculty —no plausible team even, and there was Forbes, with the conviction, the drive and the intelligence. Nothing further is needed to explain how he came to play so decisive a part and was discovered, in those first post-Armistice terms, when the demobilized rapidly refilled Cambridge and inquiries multiplied into what 'English' might mean, *being* it—being the new opportunity in person.

Of course, he incidentally reinforced some conceits and exposed his influence to the charge of inspiring and equipping ambitious stupidities and stark insensibilities to posture as something else. But what 'teacher' can be ensured against that kind of hazard? Where does safety lie—unless in nullity? We didn't need Nietzsche to tell us to live dangerously; there is no other way of living. Forbes, himself a vital force of intelligence, had, in the strong disinterested way, the courage of life and, it follows, the impulse and the power to stir intelligence into active life in others.

That is what he did. It was the favour of the gods that gave such a start to Cambridge English. A good proportion of the undergraduates were proper 'university material', capable of responding to the exemplification of what a genuine interest in creative works was like and how perception and judgment might be developed into critical thought. They got from him what they couldn't have got from the server-up of Oliver Elton or of Bradley and Raleigh or from the belletristic product of Classics. Forbes at Cambridge had read History. It came between him and whatever he may have had of Public School Classics: his adult literary interests developed spontaneously and strongly among the widely diverse interests of his adult intellectual life, and he hadn't to emancipate himself from the confirmed conventionalities of 'educated' taste, but could take with spirited freedom the opportunity the new tripos was for him—for the 'teacher' himself as collaborative learner.

His 'eccentricity' was to a great extent nothing worse than idiosyncratic vivacity, and was not for that the less valuable as a provocation to critical reactions in the student when it manifested itself in the extravagant forms that were bound to be questioned. The essential vivacity that made Forbes so effective in his role of awakener of intelligence and the power of perceptive response is suggested by this, the last of the 'protocols' quoted by I. A. Richards in the section of *Practical Criticism* devoted to Poem V (Edna St Vincent Millay's sonnet):

> This is a studied orgasm from a 'Shakespeare-R. Brooke' complex, as piece 7 from a 'Marvell-Wordsworth-Drink-water, etc., stark-simplicity' complex. Hollow at first reading; resoundingly hollow at second. A sort of thermos vacuum, 'the very thing' for a dignified picnic in this sort of Two-Seater Sonnet. The '*Heroic*' *Hectoring* of line 1, the hearty *quasi*-stoical button-holing of the unimpeachably-equipped beloved, *the magisterial finger-wagging* of 'I tell you this'!! Via such conduits magnanimity may soon be laid on as an indispensable, if not obligatory, modern convenience.[1]

It should go on record that it was Forbes who determined and contrived Richards's association with Cambridge English, having made it, as a beneficent one, possible. In fact, in the days of its importance—or the phase of it that entitles Richards to his place in this history—the association with Cambridge English was inseparable from an association with Forbes. The 'protocol' I have just quoted would be a good text for enlarging on this delicate theme. Richards himself couldn't have written anything as lively and to the point—as anyone can see who reads through the 'practical' part of *Practical Criticism*. I put 'practical' in inverted commas because the relation between Richards's play with the 'protocols' and the intelligent practice of criticism, or practical incitement to it, has always seemed to me so indeterminate (it seems carefully that) and so questionable. His own

---

[1] *Practical Criticism*, page 79.

interest in literature was not intense and was never developed.

Nevertheless, his part in the alliance with Forbes that established as a recognized thing the need to cultivate sensibility in a discipline of intelligence directed upon words, rhythm and 'imagery'—language in its poetically creative use—was necessary. He had the ability and the will to impress reassuringly the aspirants to power, the academico-political rivals for whom the instituting of the Faculty system in 1927 provided inevitable opportunities —which they inevitably took. The initiating critical intelligence, the intelligence that is sensibility and goes only with intense disinterested interest in literature and percipience in the face of actual creative effects, was Forbes's. Richards's intrinsically valuable contribution is represented by the strong element in his earlier book, *Principles of Literary Criticism*. It was a not so very common kind of commonsense intelligence which shows to advantage in the chapters on 'Rhythm and Metre' and 'Poetry for Poetry's Sake'. The benefit it conferred was liberation. To be released from the thought-frustrating spell of 'Form', 'pure sound value', prosody and the other time-honoured quasi-critical futilities had a positively vitalizing effect that can hardly be done justice to today. The fact that the insistent pretension of the book was the pseudo-scientific pseudo-psychological, representing the other association—C. K. Ogden and Neo-Benthamism, and that it was that which gave the book its notoriety and the enemies of intelligence their excuse for dismissing 'Cambridge Criticism', mattered comparatively little. It was not a paradox that the only serious criticism the pseudo-science had was the product of Cambridge English.

Where you have, working under real university conditions, and authorized by a charter such as the English Tripos provided, students of university quality who enjoy some measure of the kind of stimulus and aid I have pointed to, then, however small the official provision of these may be, the thing has been done, the creative innovation achieved, the new forms of life established. So, looking back at the pre-war decade, I was able, in the 'Retrospect' that accompanied the reprinted *Scrutiny*, to say:

> Cambridge, then, figured for us civilization's anti-Marxist recognition of its own nature and needs—recognition of that, the essential, which Marxian wisdom discredited, and the external and material drive of civilization threatened, undoctrinally, to eliminate. It was our strength to be, in our consciousness of our effort, and actually, in the paradoxical and ironical way I have to record, representatives of that Cambridge. We *were*, in fact, that Cambridge: we felt it, and had more and more reason to feel it, and our confidence and courage came from that. In the strength of the essential Cambridge which it consciously and explicitly represented, *Scrutiny* not only survived the hostility of the institutional academic powers, it became—who now question it?—the clear triumphant justification to the world of Cambridge as a humane centre.

Only at Cambridge could *Scrutiny* have been conceived, launched and carried on. It was the justifying product of the English Tripos, and, in being the kind of enterprise it was, it implicitly insisted on a conscious realization that Cambridge English was pre-eminently the representative of a distinctive Cambridge tradition, to vindicate which in modern terms was to assert, re-conceived in relation to a rapidly changing world, the Idea of the

University. Of course, what I said in the 'Retrospect', and what I say now, isn't properly modest. But proper modesty is out of place where issues so momentous are in question. I have to enforce concerning those issues convictions that I know to be well founded, and *Scrutiny* is an essential part of the history, the evidence and the argument. It is there, readily accessible, to be examined, and its significance, for those who are capable of real solicitude about the issues, is plain.

It is a significance that, contemplated from the present, has its poignancy, for the promise that might have seemed to be inherent in it has been defeated, and the suggestion of hope can only be seen as an irony. It could hardly be a sanguine hope even in the nineteen-thirties—at any rate for those actually engaged at Cambridge in the struggle to keep *Scrutiny* alive. They were not persons of academic consequence, and those who had the power and the influence in the English Faculty were not disposed to recognize the significance in question, or to countenance it if they saw it. Richards settled down to re-stating Coleridge in terms of Bentham and propaganding Basic English (enterprises that were not calculated to alarm the rising academic powers[1]), and Forbes withdrew into the background and died in 1936.

The continuation of the history at this point presents some delicacy, and I am glad to take advantage of the aid incidentally provided by a reviewer in the *Times Literary Supplement* that has just come (April 25, 1968). The two volumes before him are those of *A Selection from Scrutiny*, and the fact that his review is highly favourable

---

[1] Cf: 'Scrutiny is very alarming'—the comment of a prepotent politician of the English School in the middle nineteen-thirties.

gives point to the comments it invites in relation to my present theme:

> If there is one general impression arising from this close-packed anthology of high criticism, it is the collective modesty of the *Scrutiny* movement. Modesty—in *Scrutiny?* Yes. The modesty of a group of high-principled and exceedingly clever critics who simply could not grasp the fact that their detractors, and the indifferent, were very much smaller fry than themselves. The famous exchanges between F. R. Leavis of *Scrutiny* and F. W. Bateson of *Essays in Criticism* on the functions of 'The Responsible Critic' fill thirty-six pages of fascinating polemics. . . . Yet it is the clobbered Mr Bateson who, in a specially contributed and generous postscript, points the moral by admitting himself (possibly ironically, but nevertheless accurately) to be 'a lesser man in an inferior English Faculty'. The Scrutineers simply could not see that other men were incapable of their own highly professional skills.

The clear goodwill of this brings out the portentous force of the incomprehension, or unawareness, it exemplifies. In attributing 'professional skill' to us, what profession has the writer in mind as that with which such skill as he praises would naturally associate? The profession of 'teacher' in a university English school?— The kind of skill represented by *Scrutiny* was not, we had the most compelling reason for being aware, regarded by the actual profession as professional. Quite the contrary; the professional spokesmen, the institutional powers and authorities, the rising young men and the recruits favoured for co-option regarded such skill as offensively *un*professional, and the practitioners as deserving to be maligned, branded, excluded and starved out. You couldn't, you can't, wage the desperate and necessary battle to vindicate life and the nature of true professional skill (this is an advantage the enemy has—

for there *is* an enemy) without being exposed to the kind of charge brought by the reviewer. Blake has some relevant observations.

'English' suffers by reason of its extreme remoteness as an academic study and a discipline from Mathematics: how produce and enforce the standards that determine genuine qualification? If the first emergent Faculty powers were unchecked mediocrities (they were) they would pack the Faculty with mediocrities, and thereafter it would be safe; to keep out the dangerous—that is, the intelligent and genuinely qualified—by unquestionable (or unquestioned) methods would be easy. It would be a simple enough matter to see that the Appointments Board was properly composed.

The reviewer writes as if the 'Scrutineers' ('a group of high-principled and exceedingly clever critics') were a privileged *élite*, practising criticism in Olympian security. Actually, everything depended on the two who are most kindly spoken of in the review. They were the permanent devoted presences that kept *Scrutiny* going, and, in the one place and the only way in which it could be done, kept the contributing connexion continually recruited and renewed (ensuring, in the course of doing it, that the pre-Faculty potentiality of creative life implicit in what I have called the 'charter' should be kept still living—to the resolutely prophylactic disgust of the new professional academics). One of the pair, my wife, has had no academic recognition of any kind since the publication of *Fiction and the Reading Public* (1932), and has recently, after a life devoted to scholarship and criticism, Cambridge English, and the service of that literary tradition which might today be this country's indisputable claim to honour, distinction and self-respect, received a final rebuff—a very pointed one. As for myself, I, by dint of activating Q's natural manly decency (he was Commodore of the Fowey Yacht Club and a gentleman) attained to an Assistant Lectureship in my forties and a full Lectureship ten years later, and was made a Reader in my sixty-fifth year. But, though the reviewer credits me with a reputation as a teacher and speaks of the *Scrutiny* team as 'high-principled and exceedingly clever critics', and they were very largely in one way or another pupils of myself and my wife, I was never on the Appointments Board, and no pupil of mine was ever appointed to a post in the Cambridge English Faculty.

The reviewer may be inclined to suggest that this (to us) in some ways depressing history was the consequence of our *not* 'ignoring, instead of castigating, the opposition to *Scrutiny*' (it included the *Times Literary Supplement*), and not setting up on our desks 'the comforting sentence: "Fret not thyself because of the evil-doers".' Surely, if we had not incurred resentment by attempting to serve the full function of criticism instead of confining ourselves to the display of our gifts for appreciating what we admired, there would not have been this exclusion? To believe this is to underrate the percipient prudence of established mediocrity—the instinctive and cultivated habit that makes it quick and decided in its reaction to the signs of disturbing intelligence, unacceptable genuineness and unaccommodating disinterestedness.

The reviewer thinks highly of the reprinted essays on Wordsworth and Metaphysical Poetry, and salutes them as classics. But the author, of whom T. S. Eliot, recalling memories of nearly twenty years back, once said to me that 'he was the most brilliant undergraduate of his time

(I read his fellowship dissertation)', was firmly told in his quite early graduate days by the all-powerful boss of the Faculty that there was no future for him in Cambridge English. This decisive and final elimination was compatible with the appointment and perpetuation of 'brilliant' charlatans, confident products of the Classical Tripos, and dull mediocrities.[1] It took place when there had been no provocative appearance in *Scrutiny*. But then the eliminated was unmistakably the kind of mind a *Scrutiny* would recruit.

Such an 'establishment' inevitably objects to a serious conception of the critical function. That is why the advice retrospectively offered by the *Times Literary Supplement* reviewer entails a failure to understand what *Scrutiny* aimed at, what it achieved, and the conditions of that part of the achievement he admires.

Our hope had been, of course, that, by keeping alive the potentiality that the foundation of the English Tripos had established—by insisting on it and enforcing in such practice as was open to us ('Scrutiny is very alarming') the implicit idea of an English School and so of a university, we might ensure that the actuality should sufficiently root itself at Cambridge to be permanently established, a robust living and developing presence at the centre, its necessity and significance recognized, its growth a matter of intelligent response to the advances of technological civilization. But the logic I have just described completed its demonstration; the 'danger', exorcized, no longer threatens the English School and

---

[1] An early friend of mine, revisiting Cambridge in the late nineteen-twenties and inquiring innocently of a Faculty power who knew us both how I was getting on, was told: 'In one sense he's doing well, and the Faculty is lucky to have him. But he won't get on—his standard is too high'.

the future is safe; Cambridge is no longer a centre of life and hope. No clear purpose or positive idea replaces what has been exorcized. Where there is no positive idea that could inform a clear, strong and disinterested purpose ambition and incuria, natural consorts, reign in security; they reign, and perhaps steer, but can hardly be said to direct—the actuality is an accelerating drift (which will become a drive) of Americanization. Cambridge, that is, exemplifies rather than resists the universal reductive process.

'The vacuity of ordinary America'—the phrase meets my eye in an article by an American student of American civilization in an American intellectual review[1] that has just come. The kind of vacuity isn't peculiarly American; it is a vacuity that technologico-Benthamite civilization is creating and establishing in this country. But there are degrees, and superior advancedness is portentously influential. The Americanization is to be fought because it is rapidly bringing us to a state as hopeless as America's—a state from which recovery seems inconceivable; we shall be able to do nothing to help ourselves, and therefore, it is important to add, nothing to help America (the realization of a responsibility here, I am reminding the reader, would be a recognizable face of recovered 'purpose'—I am thinking of the 'sense of purpose' the loss of which is so generally deplored). For this country still has advantages: I mention on a later page[2] the Americans who deplore the determination shown by our enlightened to incur a further loss—to throw away the advantage we have in the field of education.

Enlightenment—the standard enlightenment of the

[1] *Commentary*. And see Appendix II.
[2] See page 181 below.

24

New Statesman, the *Guardian*, clergymen and Members of Parliament—is a formidable aspect of the menace we have to defeat. It will certainly be met with in any university. I have found myself confronted by it at the close of a discussion-opening talk addressed to a picked audience—graduates, an Education Officer, two or three schoolmasters, representatives of Social Studies—in a Department of Education. My tactical assumption of a general concurrence in my sketch of the world in which schoolmasters have to do their work was not endorsed— I had in front of me an ostensible unanimity of dis- approval, indignant and unconcessive, though (I thought) quaking—not with pure indignation.

This last note as I intend it takes the emphasis. The purpose of a realistic contemplation of the disaster over- taking humanity is not to induce pessimism but resolu- tion, and the resolution called for is one intelligent and grounded. My 'quaking' registers the perception that my enlightened audience, with resentful unwillingness, recognized as portentous facts the facts I pointed to, and half-recognized that their blankness in face of the significance was refusal. The head of 'student unrest', though adduced by me, received no attention—the phenomenon at the given university had been a major nuisance, irrationally and recklessly damaging, wholly gratuitous, and, in the fatuous pretensions that gave it its show of active virtue and competent maturity, too menacing a portent to be condonable or merely risible. Wanton destructiveness had also been a cause of concern at the university: no one took that theme up, or chose to discuss the significance of the now rooted and still spreading drug habit. Evasiveness prevailed and took the place of discussion. My asking whether they thought that, when America had solved the race problem and achieved something like our Welfare State, America, so immensely the richer and more powerful, would be happy served only to release some exalted, irrelevant and depressing unrealities about the immigrant-problem here. As for the revolution in the matter of sex, the manifest tendency was to deny that there had been a revolution, and to question in a knowing way whether things had ever been different.

The flagrant facts are so familiar to all in universities, or schools, or social work, or medicine, or anywhere, that to meet my indelicate insistence on them a defensive tactic was ready. It was to invoke the desirability of experimentation and to praise the candour of the young. 'Candour', I pointed out (I can leave 'experimentation' without comment now), meant irresponsibility, confident ignorance, levity and callousness, and the use of the word in this way was a characteristic mark of enlightenment— the enlightenment that is the deadly enemy, being itself the irresponsibility, righteously practising connivance in the interest (whether it knows it or not) of self-indulgent ease.[1]

I mustn't be taken to report the whole company

---

[1] E.g. The current issue (2 August 1968) of the *New Statesman*, supremely the organ of orthodox enlightenment, prints this in its 'This England' feature:

'I know of a very decent little student, who, because she refused to go to bed with any Tom, Dick or Harry of the men students, had to put up with being referred to as "The Virgin Mary" by these oversexed, rate-robbing, tax-robbing, so-called students.'

It isn't the contributor who is exposed for ironic contemplation—he gets a prize. The function of 'This England' is to assure the *New Statesman* reader that he belongs to an élite of the enlightened who can smile with easy superiority at out-of-date and stuffy prudery, priggishness, puritanism and hypocrisy (or 'convention').

present as coming under this description. There were members of the university who saw more point in watching the demonstration achieve its simple significant perfection than in intervening—my perception to that effect was confirmed afterwards. These represented that element which the creative effort must depend upon everywhere, and which—whether in strength enough or not is another matter—it would be reasonable to count on finding in any university. They were qualified to collaborate in enforcing and demonstrating the essential positive reply (which I didn't attempt to make) to the one clear challenge that was thrown out—I didn't attempt the positive reply because, in the measure the given conditions permitted, I had already made it in my address. The challenge was: 'You seem to think that social reform is not enough!' 'I do think that,' I answered; 'that is just what I have been trying to make plain.' In answering so I put 'social' mentally in inverted commas: the battle against enlightenment is the battle to assert and vindicate a profounder conception of 'society' than the technologico-Benthamite world knows. For to call attention as one does in waging that battle to the way in which a language exists—has its life and maintains it in constant creative renewal—is to invoke (as I point out below[1]) more than an analogy of the collaborative-creative continuity that is the presence and life of a culture.

There is the answer here to the kind of criticism represented by the writer (he was an American—but British writers have invoked him approvingly) who recently intimated that contemplating Dachau and Buchenwald and the evidence that persons of fine

[1] See page 49.

literary culture could countenance such unspeakable inhumanities made him question the efficaciousness, the humane virtue, ascribed by me to literary education. I don't find that kind of criticism very formidable but I have noticed the curious way in which modes of comment that seem to me merely unintelligent are taken up and become currency—this one has been approved and repeated. (And did not the late Aldous Huxley invent the term 'literarism' in order to attribute to me a vice that should balance against Lord Snow's 'scientism'?) Let me then say, for the benefit of the reviewer who may look through these introductory pages and, perhaps, find his eye arrested by a firm and clear statement in the close, that my preoccupation in the following lectures (or anywhere else) is not of the kind such criticism might have led him to assume.

It is not with the advocacy of a university English school that should send out into the world a number of discriminating critics and a greater number of cultivated readers: to make it that—merely that—is to denature it. And it is not with merely literary education (whatever 'merely literary' might mean—I address the reviewer)[1].

[1] He might (e.g.) be the writer of the résumé-commentary on the opening page of the issue (July 25, 1968) of the *Times Literary Supplement* devoted to 'The Teaching of English Literature'. At the bottom of the fourth column we read this:

'it is difficult in these days to talk with any ringing confidence about the "civilizing" benefits to be derived from a study of great authors. If the Arnoldian-Leavisite position, which in a sense represents literature's last-ditch attempt to claim for itself a distinct social function, really does have to be abandoned, then English studies may very well find themselves in a perilous position. Once it is conceded that literature is worth study for its own sake, that it is as misleading to boast of its morally nutritive properties as it is to mutter that it's all to do with palaeography, some tender flanks will be exposed.'

Nor is it merely with education. It is with restoring to this country an educated public that shall be intelligent, conscious of its responsibility, qualified for it and influential—such a public as might affect decisively the

The confident and unconscious incapacity for thought exposed here is depressingly familiar—and probably Oxford, for all the writer leaves himself to stand for is an indolent complacency of belles-lettres and Oxford 'civilization'. Without accepting the assimilation of my position to Arnold's, I can ask on behalf of us both: 'What *is* studying literature for its own sake?' The writer's phrase depends for the illusion that it means something on the insinuation conveyed by 'literature's last-ditch attempt to claim for itself a distinct social function'. The insinuation is that Arnold and myself, neither of whom respects the aestheticism of Art for Art's Sake, *therefore* stand convicted of misusing literature in the ways typified by Marxist 'interpretation' and the symbol industry. 'Literature for Literature's Sake' may not seem so exposed a formula as 'Art for Art's Sake'—but what *is* literature? Clive Bell (also the author of *Civilisation*), who in *Art* carried aestheticism to its high point of sophistication, defines visual art as 'Significant Form', inviting the comment that he really means 'Non-significant', since (he contends) Pure Art Value, or pure aesthetic experience, which is what you get if you appreciate art as art, is *sui generis* and can't be related or intelligently discussed: you can only ejaculate (meaning no more than 'Oh!' or 'Ah!' or 'Gosh!') But a literary work is composed of language and language is nothing if not concerned with meanings, and 'Form' in a work of literature can only be a matter of significance such as can be intelligently and profitably discussed, the discipline of criticism being a discipline for relevance in discussion and comment. Since if men were not both individuals and, as such, inescapably social beings too there would be neither language nor literature, relevant comment may very well deal in explicitly social significances. But my (and Arnold's) critic subscribes innocently to the current restrictive conception of 'social' and 'society', which is pathological in the Marxist, technologico-Benthamite and enlightened way. It is all in keeping—and unscrupulous too, for he at least makes a show of having read me—that he reduces my criticism and my advocacies to a preoccupation with 'the "civilizing" benefits to be derived from the study of great authors.'

This kind of criticism gives us what essentially enlightenment comes to. It reduces society to terms of mechanism and literature and art to causes that Lord Robbins can put in a condescending word for. (See page 172 below.)

intellectual and spiritual climate in which statesmen and politicians form their ideas, calculate, plan and perform.[1] It conceives the university not merely as a place of learning, research and instruction, but as itself a nucleus (one of a number) of the greater public, the spiritual community the country needs as its mind and conscience. I use the word 'spiritual' as a way of indicating that association of knowledge and political purpose with non-material ends and other-than-quantitative standards the lack of which makes the prospects for human life in this country (and elsewhere) so desolating.

It gave me something of the pleasure of hearing conception and faith endorsed when at a board-meeting in one of our new universities a member, answering an

[1] At a recent by-election I attended the public meeting assembled in order that the Liberal candidate (for whose nomination I had given my signature and to whose election fund I had subscribed) might be introduced to the electors. Mr Jeremy Thorpe began his introductory speech by telling us, in a sentence, that the Liberal Party stood for Comprehensive Schools—and that subject was out of the way: no more was said about education. The candidate, a successful businessman (he had made his money out of caravans, I gathered) opened with businesslike down-rightness: 'What we need is to get this country going.' Explaining the earnest practicality with which he meant this, he went on: 'When you return me next week—as you will!—I shall lay out a map of the region, I shall mark my points of growth, and I shall draw my lines of communi-cation accordingly.' We all understood that the City of Cambridge was to be a main point of growth. I myself recalled that the previous Liberal candidate, who was a good deal more like an educated man, had, in answering questions, assured his audience that there was no danger of his showing tenderness towards the University. It was plain that he naïvely assumed an antagonism between the University and the City, and, though (or because) a member of the University, was anxious not to be suspected of any but pure 'democratic' sympathies—which were (everyone knew) City.

Politicians must aim at winning elections. And I have been forced to abandon the illusion that I could show my sense of political responsibility by believing, or trying to believe, in any party.

objection to the effect that 'before we decide *that* we must find out what the country wants', said: '*We* are the country; in this matter it's we who decide—it's *our* function'. I have moved here from 'university' to 'universities'; there are now a good many of them, and the plurality was implied in the retort. We necessarily have our misgivings about some obvious consequences of the rapid multiplication; the more pressingly must we insist on what should be recognized as its essential meaning— the inherent *social* significance. We must insist that, however, little the instigators, planners and political agents of the multiplication have propounded, or *could* have propounded, the necessary new conception of the university, the conception represents—it is—the essential inherent meaning; it is the answer to humanity's *ahnung* of its profound and desperate need—the need that is the product of advanced industrial civilization.[1] There is no other answer; only in the university can the needed new function develop its organ.

[1] The desperateness of the need gets a very impressive recognition in J. K. Galbraith's *The New Industrial State*. Since Galbraith is an American economist reporting on America it would have been a miracle if, intelligent as he is, he had been able to enforce his diagnosis by prescribing a remedy more adequate to the disease and accordant to its nature than suggested new mechanisms. I take this word from the review in the *New Statesman* (27 October 1967). I will quote from that review, since the *New Statesman's* characteristic approach isn't suspect of bias in my direction.

'Having interpreted the working of the industrial system Galbraith draws some chief conclusions after which follow his recommendations. Contrary to the established liberal doctrine it is no longer possible to accept the view that individual choice is the guiding force in the economic system. ... Galbraith is not concerned primarily with the vast and growing expenditure of resources on advertising. He is not saying that advertising can sell anything, or that it corrupts some original "true" taste. Much advertising is highly competitive

'Answer' implies answerers; it can only be a matter of collaborative human effort, impelled by a vivid realization of the issues, and sustained by clear purpose and tireless pertinacity. It will depend upon strong conviction in a minority—a very small minority to begin with. But a genuine demonstrative start somewhere would have a disproportionate effect. It is surely not hopelessly unrealistic to see the possibility of such a start at one of the new universities—a start that should establish a real

and self-cancelling in its effects. The significant point is that advertising taken as a whole, as an institution, acts to mould the kind of man required by the goals of the industrial system, the kind of man that can be counted on to spend reliably and to work reliably. Once the already wealthy members of society are convinced of the need for more goods, and yet more goods, the growth of G.N.P. is accepted as an obvious aim of economic policy and the primary measure of social achievement:

'St. Peter is assumed to ask applicants only what they have done to increase G.N.P.

And not only is this prepossession with maintaining G.N.P. responsible for the relative neglect of the aesthetic dimension of life. . . .'

I can't put my finger on this last phrase in Galbraith's book, but it is good *New Statesman* and, I'll venture, good Lord Robbins. And it doesn't suggest a more serious inadequacy of recognition in Galbraith's book than is actually there. For this summary (the *New Statesman's* again) seems to me unexceptionable:

'In conclusion, Galbraith asserts the need for a mechanism to promote the neglected aspects of life, to initiate a variety of much needed public services, to promote long-term planning of urban centres, to provide employment options offering more leisure and longer vacations rather than more "real" income: in short, to provide a range of socially important choices beyond that offered by the industrial system.'

Galbraith's own account of the portentous total mechanism of American civilization makes his prescription look like a polite gesture in face of an appalling and incurable disease. And the British reader will reflect that we, in this country, *have* the Welfare State—and are assiduously emulating the disastrous characteristics of American education.

centre of life. That this was being seriously attempted would most certainly get prompt and wide recognition, to the immense advantage of the given university, which would have begun to assume a recognized importance as a focal centre and a centre of influence—perhaps decisively, so urgent is the need and so general the sense of it: the demonstration and the incitement would beyond all question tell.

I think I have made it clear that hope of this kind is very remote from easy optimism. The note of it is: 'This battle, desperate as the odds look, must not—shall not—be lost'. What threatens us, the alternative to successful resistance, is too unspeakably repellent—the hope is the recognition of that. What we face in immediate view is a nightmare intensification of what Arnold feared. He saw this country in danger of becoming a greater Holland; we see it unmistakably turning with rapid acceleration into a little America. By 'greater' Arnold meant bigger; what he feared was the relative loss of that which had made England great—as distinguished from rich, materially prosperous and powerful. What we see now in the rapid assimilation of this country to America is the jettisoning of all that made it no more paradoxical that England should have produced English Literature than that America should be producing the American literature that American wealth is bestowing on the world and American prestige recommending. We see in fact a blind and complacent acceptance of the process by which this country is ceasing to maintain its cultural continuity or to have a constitutive character at all—to be anything more (final triumph of spiritual Philistinism) than a political, economic and administrative identity.

I am not for a moment suggesting that the process can

be decently charged against America—that the disease is to be diagnosed as inflicted upon us from outside by infection or contagion. It is inherent in industrial civilization, and what I am calling attention to in these lectures is the need for a corrective provision, a sustained effort of an unprecedented kind, on the part of society—or civilized mankind. For obvious reasons the process is more advanced in America; and the way in which American influence accelerates it in this country evidences a cultural decay here that is already far advanced. Pop Art is what it is, and the masses respond to what they 'want', or recognize as irresistible. At what are ostensibly the higher cultural levels American influence tells more subtly, and it is there that we have to fight it—essentially contemptible as the manifestations are. I am thinking of the way in which it has become current as matter of commonplace that 'it's in America that the things [creative] are being done', that in literary criticism America has an obvious superiority, that American work in scholarship and criticism has in our time performed the major service to English literature.[1]

The significance of these positions lies in their being so utterly ungrounded: the British bias where literary-intellectual orthodoxy is concerned is strongly American; it exhibits our enlightened as blindly and wilfully hostile to their own country's clear and essential advantage. For (it is necessary to insist) this country still has advantages. The determination to defend and vindicate them has nothing of the chauvinist in it and is a very different

[1] The truth is that even the most acclaimed critical work on English authors—Jane Austen, the Brontës, Dickens, George Eliot, D. H. Lawrence—betrays a disqualifying ignorance of the civilization out of which those authors wrote, and thus an inability to read them. The truth holds from Edmund Wilson downwards.

thing from patriotic nationalism. Nor has the spirit of it
the least touch of compensatory nostalgia for lost imperial
'greatness'. It is time indeed for a clear recognition that
the world has changed, and that imperial 'greatness'
cannot be 'great' in the old way. Bigness, wealth and
brute power in our world are starkly bigness, wealth
and brute power, and it isn't only America, with its
strong tradition of generous idealism, that finds prepotence appearing, in a way not foreseen a decade ago,
paradoxically and embarrassingly impotent. And the
basic problem of industrial civilization won't be solved
by any kind of New Deal or by any scheme of 'participation'.

The country that should distinguish itself by a real
and sustained effort to solve it and a degree of success
that made its nature and the nature of any solution plain
would have achieved a distinction more real, more grati-
fyingly recognized and in itself more satisfying than those
which are commonly aspired to in the name of national
glory. There can be no national greatness where there is
no strong spiritual continuity—strong with the strength
of continuous renewal by re-creation. I am not forgetting
that there are still immense changes in front of us and
that the place and distinctiveness of the national entity
won't be forever what they are. But no change that can
be foreseen or feared will make the kind of effort to
keep renewed and strong the life and authority that
belong to—that *are* for us—the 'third realm', less
important, less imperative.

I
Literature and the University: the Wrong Question

LITERATURE
AND THE UNIVERSITY:
THE WRONG QUESTION

ENGLISH literature in our time—I am concerned in these lectures with that. If I had said 'in *my* time' it would have tended to have a different effect. For there have been great and rapid changes in the last forty years. This fact is an essential consideration for my particular theme, though not, perhaps, in the way I may be immediately taken to intimate: what would ordinarily be suggested by 'literary history' is not my proposed business.

Change is insisted on in this passage from the front page of the *Times Literary Supplement* for May 19, 1966 —a passage that is a pregnant text for me, inviting me to define positively the nature of my preoccupation:

'It seems inconceivable that higher education could be both a large system and a comprehensive one, and yet universities remain essentially the same as they have been; indeed there is a lack of historical perspective about Lord Robbins's comments that implies an idea of an eternal university, that belies the evidence of rapid social change in their students—and their teachers. As for their other function, have universities always been the source of the best ideas in our civilization? Name a great novelist who was a don; apart from Housman, most poets, I think, have been outside the university net?'

The article is a review of the report of the Franks Commission and of Lord Robbins's *The University and the Modern World*, a collection of his addresses. I don't want to defend Lord Robbins, and I should have liked to be able to say that my sympathies were with the reviewer, who is critical of Lord Robbins's assumptions and mode of thought. But I can't. The whole article is depressingly documentary—words the force of which (I mean the last two) will have come out, I hope, before long. It confirms my sense of the great need there is to get attention for the considerations I want to put forward —and it makes me feel (as I have felt from time to time during the last forty years) that I would rather discuss the function of the university with a mathematician or a physicist than with an academic humanist, which is what I take the reviewer to be.

The aspect of change represented by the passage I have quoted that I want to emphasize regards the latter part of it, and it is one of which the author is unconscious:

> Have universities always been the source of the best ideas in our civilization? Name a great novelist who was a don; apart from Housman, most poets, thinkers and creators have been outside the university net.

It is no new thing for an academic humanist to be blind and blank and urbanely unconcerned in that way. What I have to dwell on is the frightening truth that the blindness and blankness and unconcern are today general. You don't, of course, settle the question, how important or unimportant have Oxford and Cambridge been to English literature in the past, by asking how many dons were great novelists or great poets and offering us Housman. You say nothing to the point. You merely show your lack of interest in the nature of a civilization, and in the conditions out of which a great literature grows and by which it is kept alive.

A literature grows out of a culture. A great poet, though he may have a profound influence on his native language by his supremely creative use of it (it developed and is kept living in creative use), didn't create it. Shakespeare had an immeasurably great influence upon English, but couldn't have done so had he not inherited in it a rich, supple and exquisitely vital language. The indebtedness of Shakespearian English to the universities (though Shakespeare was notoriously *not* a classical or an English don) was immense—a subject on which a first-year man reading 'English' could write at least a page or two, and which a maturer student of distinguished mind, choosing it for a piece of original work, could make very much more of than a language specialist—or a linguis-tician—is likely (I believe) to have provided for in his implicit canons of relevance, or to be predisposed to applaud, or to see the point of.

I will say no more on this head—and I have said nothing about the University Wits. I will only add that, not merely to Shakespeare, but to the subsequent crea-tors of modern English literature it has mattered in most vital ways (and not merely materially) that England con-tained an educated class and an educated public. No one will contend that the universities had nothing to do with *their* existence.

The points I have made are obvious. I don't for a moment suggest that the writer in the *Times Literary Supplement* is inclined to question them, or to question that Oxford and Cambridge have had the greatest importance in English life and civilization. What I am calling attention to is the portentous significance of his being, when taking part in the debate, which isn't merely theoretical, about the urgent need to expand, multiply and modernize the universities, able to dismiss with such unconscious irresponsibility all suggestion that the universities have had a vital function in relation to English literature. In doing that—this is the truth for which I aim at getting a full and real recognition—he is lightly dismissing the function that, in our world (which becomes every year more completely what it is), only the university can perform. 'Lightly' is the word: his article is an unconscious tribute to the potency of the technologico-Benthamite climate in which we live. The function of the university towards the sciences will in any case be performed—provision for *them* is in no danger of being neglected: the humane function, that which gives the sciences their human meaning and their *raison d'être*, can be left to—what? The Sunday papers? If the idea of the university is not understood in the university itself, and is not fought for, with fierce, informed and resolute conviction there, where in our world will it be, and by whom?

I have perhaps made it plain by now that my associated insistences—on the university and on English literature —are two emphases in the expression of the same basic concern. It is the concern that it was Arnold's distinction to have given expression to and that makes the conception of the function of criticism he stands for—*he* made it part of the English-speaking cultural heritage—a significant development. Contemplating, in an earlier phase of it than ours, the advance of industrial civilization, he saw that something new was happening to humanity, and that England and America in especial were exposed to a new kind of menace. It is that which he has in mind when he expresses his fear that England will become a 'greater Holland'. This is obviously a recoil from triumphant materialism, affluent and unleavened. Whether or

not the way of expressing it is fair to Holland, there can
be no doubt about the essential nature of the fear; the
Arnoldian context—the immediate one and the general
context of essays and pamphlets—makes it perfectly
plain. It is that the massive and rapid growth of material
civilization, the changes in human habit and the human
condition brought about by technological advance, will
entail a lapse of that creatively human response to
economic fact, to the inescapable exigencies of life and
material circumstance, which a cultural tradition *is*—is,
while it remains a living power in the present.

Arnold saw, and said, that to preserve continuity—
continuity of cultural consciousness—a more conscious
and deliberate use of intelligence was needed than in the
past. This is the meaning of the stress he laid upon
poetic tradition (literature for him *was* poetry), and of
his preoccupation with 'centrality', with defining the idea
of 'authority' in matters of taste and judgment, and with
standards. If we are inclined to comment that his prescription, for all his command of urbane irony, looks
pathetically unrealistic in relation to the menace it has in
view, we should remind ourselves of a difference between
his time and ours that we tend to forget: in the England
he was addressing there was a large and immensely
influential educated class. He himself comments on this
fact explicitly, as well as implying everywhere his awareness of it, and his reliance on it. But, as his work in the
field of education and such essays as that on 'Equality'
testify, he was far from resting in a complacent ease of
mind about the cultural advantage England enjoyed in
the existence of this social class which shared (he accepted
for his purpose that description) the education and
manners of the governing class, and—or, if you like, and

yet—supported the Victorian intellectual reviews. He was too generous and fastidious humanly to be satisfied, and, moreover, with his eye on the inevitable coming economic, social and political transformations, he saw the dangers inherent in that ambiguity, the 'educated class' —or 'educated classes'.

It was the main concern of his life to promote in this country the steps and the process that should create (this being their ideal aim) a class of the educated—a class that could be definable and thought of as essentially and unequivocally that, in dissociation from the idea of social privilege, or social privilege as ordinarily cried out against, detested and prized (even by Lord Snow). Or perhaps it would be better to say, not thought of as class at all—though it is well to insist that there must be a community of the 'educated' that can never be a majority. No one minds—even in America—there being an *élite* of athletes. To be both brief and unambiguous in this matter is difficult, and perhaps I had better add to what I have said that Arnold had no designs *against* the actual 'educated class' that had produced him and his ideals, and that mattered so much to him and made it possible for him to energize with hope. It mattered so much because it represented the possibility of an effective appeal to standards. And what I mean by this has so essential an importance for my theme that I must now, even at the cost of some insistence on what ought to be truism—and at the cost of saying what some here will have heard me say before, try to make it plain, if I can, beyond any misunderstanding. In that attempt I have a more difficult task than Arnold had—or, perhaps I had better say, was conscious of having.

The word 'standards' is not the less necessary because,

like so many of the most important words in our field of discourse, its use can't be justified by the kind of definition the prompt logic of the enemy demands. One can't long discuss the study of literature and the unavoidableness of critical judgments *without* using it. And when I try to explain what 'standards' are, what is their nature and authority as we, students of literature and (therefore) critics, are concerned with them, my underlying and essential preoccupation is not merely or mainly theoretical, but brings together very intimately my disquiet at the actual state of criticism in the English-speaking world, my conception of what literary studies should be at the university, and my sense of the idea of a university as it needs to be fostered—and realized—in the technological age.

How, then, when the question of 'standards'—the challenge to explain what they are, or the problem of exorcizing misconceptions—comes up in the way in which it does come up for the literary critic, how as a literary critic does he deal with it? How, as a literary critic, should he deal with it?

In this insistence on 'literary critic' I have a reason: I wish to intimate that I am not proposing to attempt a philosophical discussion. I'm not much interested in establishing in any thorough-going theoretical way that the phrase 'the standards of literary criticism', means something; that their basis must be this, and their nature that. On the other hand, I *am* very much preoccupied with vindicating literary criticism as a specific discipline —a discipline of intelligence, with its own field, and its own approaches within that field. And in particular I am preoccupied with insisting that there is an approach to the problem of 'standards' that is proper to the field of literary criticism and to the literary critic as such—that you don't need to be a philosopher to make it.

Let me add at once that with this preoccupation goes —as, when it is seriously entertained, there must, I think, go—a concern for the critical function in contemporary actuality; for the function of criticism as, in sum, it is performed or not performed, and as it ought to be performed, here in our day in England. I indicate here one aspect of the difficulty of dealing with the problem of standards: you can neither separate it off, nor deal with it in the abstract. You can't profitably discuss the standards of criticism apart from the purposes and the methods, or apart from the actual functioning of criticism in the contemporary world. And apart from the ability to arrive at intelligent and sensitive judgments in the concrete—except, that is, as informed by critical experience—understanding of the nature of critical judgment in the abstract can amount to little. To consider the nature of 'standards' involves considering the function of criticism in the full sense of that phrase, and apart from intelligence about the actual functioning in the world as we know it (where, that is, we have the closest access to the concrete), that consideration will hardly achieve a living strength, the strength of real understanding. Real understanding in fact, can't be a mere theoretical matter; it will entail real critical engagement in relation to the contemporary scene.

I am emboldened to say elementary things when I remember—and I remember because the pronouncement was directed against me and an endeavour, in which I was involved, to ensure that there should be a play of serious criticism upon the contemporary scene, that not so very long ago an Editor of the *Times Literary Supplement* pronounced, in a British Council publication: 'There is ... no desirable life of the mind of which literary reviews are an essential component, and in which fixed standards of criticism gain a kind of legal backing.' To emphasize the force of 'fixed standards' he spoke also of 'imposing accepted values'—and spoke as if that were something I myself notoriously advocated. No one, then, who knows what 'standards' are and what is the nature of critical authority *could* talk of 'fixed standards' or of 'providing them with a legal backing', and no one who understands the nature of a judgment could talk of 'imposing accepted values'. Essentially, as I've said before (I suppose) in a good many places—but the point has to be made and much hangs on it, a critical judgment has the form, 'This is so, isn't it?'. And the concurrence appealed for must be real, or it serves no critical purpose, and, if he suspects insincerity or mere politeness, can bring no satisfaction to the critic—to the critic *as* critic.

What, of its very nature, the critical activity aims at, in fact, is an exchange, a collaborative exchange, a corrective and creative interplay of judgments. For though my judgment asks to be confirmed and appeals for agreement that the thing is *so*; the response I expect at best will be of the form, 'Yes, but—', the 'but' standing for qualifications, corrections, shifts of emphasis, additions, refinements. The process of personal judgment from its very outset, of course, is in subtle ways essentially collaborative, as my thinking is—as any use of the language in which one thinks and expresses one's thoughts *must* be. But the functioning of criticism demands a fully overt kind of collaboration. Without a many-sided real exchange—the implicitly and essentially collaborative interplay by which the object, the poem (for example) in which the individual minds meet, and, at the same time, the judgments concerning it, are established, the object, which we think of as 'there' in a public world for common contemplation, isn't really 'there'.

What, under the head of Practical Criticism, we call analysis is a creative, or re-creative, process. It's a more deliberate following-through of that process of creation in response to the poet's words (a poem being in question) than any serious reading is. It is a re-creation in which, by a considering attentiveness, we ensure a more than ordinary faithfulness and fulness. And actually when one is engaged in analysis one is engaged in discussion, even if only implicitly. That is a point I made in saying that a judgment has the form, 'This is so, isn't it?' One is engaged in discussion of . . .?—the poem, which is there *for* discussion only in so far as those discussing have each recreated it.

The discussion is an effort to establish the poem as something standing in a common world between those discussing, and thus to justify our habitual assumption that it does so stand. It's 'there' only when it's realized in separate minds, and yet it's not merely private. It's something in which minds can meet, and our business is to establish the poem and meet in it. Merely private, on the one hand, and, on the other, public in the sense that it can be produced in a laboratory, or tripped over— the poem is neither: the alternatives are not exhaustive. There is a third realm, and the poem belongs to that. I take courage for this reminder, for this repetition, for this insistence on the elementary, because, as I hope to bring out with the appropriate cogency—it's at any rate the purpose of these lectures, a great deal more than literary criticism is involved, just as the *rationale* of literary criticism involves a great deal more than this term itself, with its limiting adjective, might seem to imply.

Also, I wanted to say: this is as far as the literary critic *qua* literary critic need go epistemologically or metaphysically. It's all very familiar—with the familiarity of things that are so fundamental, so necessarily taken for granted, that we don't ordinarily bother to recognize them. If difficulty should seem to be caused by the demand for full conscious recognition (which is necessary when it's a question of justifying the pretensions of criticism, and the implicit pretensions of literature and art in general, and all mature interest in literature and art) the critic can say: 'But consider language.' A language—apart from the conventional signs and symbols for it—is really *there*, it really exists in full actuality, only in individual users; it is *there* only as its idioms, phrases, words and so on, with the meaning, intention, force in which their life resides, are uttered and meant by me (for example) and taken by you. Do they then belong to the public world (you can't point to them), or are they merely personal and private? We know that the brisk 'either-or' doesn't meet the case.

And language, in the full sense, in the full concrete reality that eludes the cognizance of any form of linguistic science, does more than provide an analogue for a 'culture' in that full sense which very much concerns us, but eludes the immense body of important people who share Lord Robbins's outlook; it is very largely the essential life of a culture. And literature, of course, is a mode or manifestation of language.

What in all this I have been trying to bring into clear

49

and full recognition is the collaborative-creative nature of criticism; and I have my eye now particularly on the word 'standards'. Criticism is concerned with establishing the poem—or the novel—as an object of common access in what is in some sense a public world so that when we differ about it we are differing about what is sufficiently the same thing to make differing profitable. But the establishing of the poem (or the novel) is the establishing of a value. Any reading of it that takes it *as* a work of art involves an element of implicit valuation. The process, the kind of activity of inner response and discipline, by which we take possession of the created work is essentially the kind of activity that completes itself in a value-judgment.

Of course, here again the enemy has his opportunity. Valuation isn't a simple idea, and the process of 'valuing' isn't in simple analogy with putting a price on. 'Value', in fact, is another of those essential words which, as needed for our purposes, don't lend themselves to the kind of definition necessary for effective defence against the indifference that, in a Benthamite and egalitarian world, so rapidly becomes overt hostility. I'm avowing that when I say that 'value' is inextricably bound up with 'significance'. And so far from valuing being a matter of bringing up a scale, a set of measures, or an array of fixed and definite criteria to the given work, every work that makes itself felt as a challenge evokes, or generates, in the critic a fresh realization of the grounds and nature of judgment. A truly great work is realized to *be* that because it so decidedly modifies—alters —the sense of value and significance that judges. That is what is testified to in the commonplace that a great artist creates the taste by which he is appreciated.

'Creates' is the right word: in the effect on the public's power to respond and realize, the effect on taste—to accept that word for the moment (though it carries a most inadequate suggestion), creative genius achieves the completion of its distinctive work. D. H. Lawrence makes that point in the answer he gave to a question put to him, very near the end of his life, about the nature of the artist's impulsion—his drive: 'One writes out of one's moral sense; for the race, as it were'. On 'moral'—and that it should carry, even for the use in which the critic finds it necessary, the odour of an unpleasant or bad word is a symptom of our time—the immediately relevant commentary again comes from Lawrence.

> The true artist doesn't substitute immorality for morality. On the contrary, he *always* substitutes a finer morality for a grosser. As soon as you see a finer morality, the grosser becomes relatively immoral.

It is when we feel that the radical criteria are notably challenged that the word 'moral' comes up; it comes up *because* they are challenged, and is our response to the realization. About Lawrence one might say that his moral perception is a manifestation of his genius, being the fineness of his sense of life—his sense of the difference between what makes *for* life and what makes against it. But to say that is to invite the comment that it is a large proposition, and 'life' is a large word. What is life? The advantage the critic enjoys when justifying such uses as he has to make of the word, and of his other indispensable terms, is that he has the work of a creative writer in front of him; he is preoccupied with referring as sensitively, faithfully and closely to that as he is able. The terms are prompted by the created thing, and he in turn gives them, for the reader, their charge of special meaning, their due specific force, by means, essentially, of a tact of particular reference to the given work as present— that is the aim—in the evoked experience of it, the evoked recall (a critical process that is, in its wholly subservient and instrumental way, itself creative).

From time to time, as I was preparing these lectures, I felt that I had overworked that last adjective and must both become more sparing of it and do some revisionary elimination. But prescription, I found, was one thing, and performance another; and, further, I found myself reflecting that my theme of its very nature entailed so much the kind of insistence directed by Blake against the cultural tyranny he associated with the names of Newton and Locke that to avoid a frequent use of the word was impossible. Blake was the human protest on behalf of life against the repression of creativity represented by the prevailing ethos of the 18th century—life, he insisted, was essentially creative in a way denied not only by the prepotence of Newton and Locke in the dominant spirit of 'civilized' and final commonsense, but by the very language—the modes and conventions of utterance—established firmly as belonging to the basic nature of things and the spirit of civilization, and accepted as natural. The emphasis Blake lays on art and the artist is one with his insistence on the creativeness of perception.

The civilization we live in presents a more formidable menace to life, and, in saying that, I see the justification of my reference to Blake in the force, peculiarly appropriate to my purpose, that the word 'life' now has, thus associated with Blake's kind of insistence on an essential creativeness—'creativeness' itself being given the right charge of meaning. The generality of my proposition has, then (I hope), for those I am addressing, the directed point and the edge it has in my own mind. The menace, the sense of its lethal insidiousness, was (as so often) borne in on me with disturbing vividness quite recently, when I listened to a paper on Newman's *Idea of a University*. The paper was distinguished, informed by wide experience, and provocative of question and comment; but, as I knew, effective discussion of fundamentals is improbable, indeed almost impossible, in a large assembly. Nevertheless, since no one, when the time for discussion came, seemed anxious to speak first, I opened by saying briefly what I most wanted to say. It was roughly this:

'I didn't, Sir, like your dividing the business of the university under two heads: one, handing things on (the word "tradition" came in here), and the other, creating new knowledge. It prejudices the upshot at the very beginning—unless challenged. What I am most concerned for that comes under your "handing things on" is rather to be called "maintaining a continuity", and perhaps I can make clear the difference I have in mind by adding immediately that for "continuity" you can substitute "a life"—"maintaining a life". Consider the life of a language: a language is maintained in *use*— use by a community in response to changing conditions and a changing civilization, and the use that maintains it is creative.'

The reader of the paper saw my point, but as I expected, it wasn't taken up in discussion. But towards the close a speaker who had shown himself notably articulate remarked, glancing back over what had been said, that I, he gathered, was a vitalist. I could only reply that I didn't see how that word helped. I felt, in fact, non-plussed; very few, it was plain, had taken my meaning, and I recognized that an attempt to convey it on that kind of occasion was an enterprise absurdly out of the question. No thought of any philosophy or intellectual system, of course, had been in my mind; I merely meant to evoke in my hearers a strong present sense of what they of course knew, and to insist on its crucial relevance.

But did they know it? Do people know it? They do and they don't. The problem of getting them to recognize it is very like the problem of getting people to recognize what they take for granted, what they implicitly assume, when they formulate and advance a critical judgment and engage in the critical discussion to which it leads.

The 'handing-on', then, for which it is recognized (in a kind of way) that provision has to be made in the conception of a new university isn't a mere matter of handing on—handing over—tools, data, inert equipment, externalities to be taken possession of as such, conquered provinces, technical know-hows. In its vital nerve (and if it hasn't one, it's nothing), and most essentially, it's a matter of carrying on a vital continuity in which the promoters and executants are already involved in such a way that, but for their being so involved, there would have been no conception, no planning, and no point in founding a university. They have, that is, a common culture in which (say), for all their differences, agnostics, Catholics and diverse kinds of Protestant can work together for common human ends. Such a cultural tradition, like the language that is at the heart of it, has been formed and kept living—that is, changing in response to changing conditions (material, economic and so on)—by continuous collaborative renewal. The participants tend to be hardly conscious of the basic values and assumptions they share, but it is the sense of something basic shared that makes possible the assumption (for instance) that there is point in founding new universities.

The state, however, of being hardly conscious, or mainly unconscious, illustrated by the episode I have just related, won't do in the civilization that sweeps us on. Without a human effort of a kind the need for which Lord Robbins and his associates have given no sign of being aware of, an effort directed and sustained by intelligent purpose, the new universities—the universities in sum—will merely be a part of the process by which, whatever provision is made for philosophy, psychology and the social sciences, the world comes to assume invincibly, to the immense impoverishment of life, that a rising 'standard of living' is a sufficient account of human ends. That is the significance of the uninhibited frankness with which Lord Robbins avows his solidarity with Lord Snow.

What, of course, I have virtually been saying is that the unprecedented civilization to which we are committed demands a new, or a more strongly positive, conception of the university and its function. The great and most menacing change brought about by the technological revolution is that it has almost destroyed the creative cultural process, of which the finer operation in that continuous renewal which maintained the human world of values and significances and spiritual graces is on the point of death; it has turned the business of human adjustment to changing material conditions into a reductive process, largely determined by business profit. The worker earns the wherewithal and the leisure to enjoy a higher standard of living by work that has little interest for him and little human meaning; it is something to be got behind him so that he can get away to live—before the telly, over the pools form, in the bingo hall, in the car. Technology, and the financial appetites, mechanisms and potencies produced by it, have determined his culture for him and saved him the trouble.

It wasn't my purpose to develop this particular branch of the theme; but I wanted to remind you that the facts it points to concern vitally, not merely the industrial workers directly affected, but all of us, including those of us whose business is with English literature—which achieved its greatness in another kind of human world. And I will now revert to that matter of 'standards', which I left hanging in the air—a matter on which, as everyone knows, the technological revolution has a bearing. The term 'standards' presents itself when there is question of getting recognition for the justice—or the absurdity—of judgments affirming (explicitly or implicitly) relative value and importance. It's a representative use, for instance, when I say that the general acceptance, in England, of Hemingway as a great writer, or the spectacle of an academic critic going out of his way to pronounce a Kingsley Amis novel a 'serious study in amorality', would have been possible only in a period marked by a collapse of standards. We talk about 'standards', in fact, at times when it is peculiarly hard to invoke standards with effect. And they can be 'there' to be invoked with effect by the critic only in the existence of an educated public capable of responding intelligently, and influential enough to make its response felt. I need say no more by way of defining standards. They depend

on, they are a manifestation of, that collaborative interplay in which the poem is established as something in
which minds can meet, which maintains the life of a
language, which creates the essential values and significances of the human world, which creates a culture.

When one speaks of the lapse of standards what one
is pointing to is the fact that it is hard for the critic to
believe in any decisive influence represented by any
public his work can be supposed to imply. It isn't that
there aren't many intelligent and cultivated persons
about, enough to be a potential influence of great value,
whose 'yes, but—', or whose 'no', is of the kind the
critic needs, but they don't form an effective public;
they don't really form a public at all.

To bring out the force of that truth one can adduce
the fact—it is at least very suggestive—that the whole
of the English-speaking world can't, or won't, maintain,
on ordinary business lines, a single serious critical
journal. The related fact is that such performance of the
current function of criticism as can be alleged is what
we see in the review pages of the weeklies and the
Sunday papers, and it certainly doesn't imply the existence of a public that entertains and exacts a serious
conception of the critical function.

The theme is one I needn't enlarge upon. The relevance
of the present alarm about the difficulty of keeping a
newspaper going on a circulation of a mere million or two
is plain. If the advance of technology and the conditions of
a technological civilization mean that a 'quality' newspaper must have an immense advertising revenue, then
the editorial policy must be one that ensures an immense
circulation, and the review-columns that make the formal
salute to literary culture will, judged as an offer to perform

the function of criticism, be contemptible. And the reviewing in the 'intellectual' weeklies will be indistinguishable in general quality from that in the Sunday papers. The same kinds of writer, very largely the same writers, write in both and are most of them in other ways actively engaged in the culture of the technological age; and as for the cultural standards of their smaller and superior public, the Sunday papers (like the review columns of the *Guardian*) in any case give us them.

Now there is no question of trying to reverse, or halt, the advance of technology. There can be no restoring the wheelwright's shop or the conditions of production that integrated work organically with a living culture and associated it in a major way with the creative human response. But that doesn't mean that we must, or should, leave the human heritage, the cultural continuity, to lapse and let technology henceforward dictate, unchecked by any human wisdom or human sense more mature than Lord Robbins's. There is a dreadful blank unconsciousness to be faced, as Lord Robbins unconsciously testifies; but there is also in humanity an instinct of self-preservation to appeal to—a sense of vital needs thwarted and starved by technologico-Benthamite civilization.

The university, in so far as it is more than a centre and nursery of the sciences, a technological institute, or a collocation of specialist departments, is the representative of that instinct, and the organ through which society has to make the sustained effort (one directed by collaborative intelligence and a full human responsibility) to keep those needs recognized and provide our civilization with memory and mature purpose. Although, as I pointed out in commenting on that odd and significant dismissive attitude of the writer in the *Times Literary*

Supplement, the university has always had a major importance in relation to the country's cultural life—an importance (the immediate emphasis) for creative literature, its function was never so vital as it is now: living continuity used to be maintained in many ways in the functioning of the general life of society—in the life of the home, for instance, and of the local milieu, and there was not that destructive action on the creative heritage and the human positive response which characterizes the mechanisms of civilization in our time—characterizes them to such a tune that, in the resulting amnesia and passivity, the destructiveness isn't recognized as such. As things are now, if provision is not made for the focused and fostered insight, purpose and effort of continuity, the heritage is lost, abandoned to oblivion, and mankind faces a fate more certain than the feared nuclear cataclysm. I recall Mr Owen Barfield's recent comment—a retort to naïve neo-Wellsian euphoria—on that transatlantic world which confronts us with our own imminent future.

> I had not thought death had undone so many

—a sentence that, with its dual context, you know. The only possible provision, the only possible organ, is the university—to recognize which fact is to recognize the context of organic life the university must have in the country at large, will draw its strength from, and will foster.

When I say that the university as a centre of consciousness for the community must have its centre in an English school, I don't mean anything of the kind that was meant when we were told, at Cambridge, forty years ago: 'Poetry will save us'. Nor do I mean that in some hierarchy of esteem English comes first. But the need is for a focal centre; and a focus of cultural continuity can only be in English. English literature, magnificent and matchless in diversity and range, and so full and profound in its registration of changing life, gives us a continuity that is not yet dead. There is no other; no other access to anything approaching a full continuity of mind, spirit and sensibility—which is what we desperately need.

II
The Present and the Past: Eliot's Demonstration

THE PRESENT AND THE PAST:
ELIOT'S DEMONSTRATION

No one, I hope, thinks I'm proposing that the university should henceforward produce English literature—or undertake to do so. I agree, it's true, that a new formulation of the idea, or a new realization, is needed, but the idea as I have it in mind doesn't involve the assumption that the university English School should teach creative writing—should suppose *that* its business or itself qualified. This is worth saying, perhaps, because so many reformers, judging by their letters to the *Times Literary Supplement* (for instance), seem to believe something of the kind. I don't at all favour the institution known as the 'creative writer on the campus' (but then I don't, for British universities, favour the 'campus'—there may be a great deal in a word). Further, I don't at all think that candidates for Honours should be encouraged to believe that by submitting original poems, novels or plays to the examiners, they may improve their claim to a good class. My reasons for this attitude had better be saved for less public circumstances; they entail, among other things, some observations I have made about modern academicism in literary matters. In any case, such a policy is not the way in which the academic in the bad sense will be defeated.

The business of the university, the focal function in this matter being the English School's, is to counter the frightening development of our civilization to which, at an earlier stage, Arnold tried to alert his countrymen. It is to replace the educated public, now decayed, that

Arnold after all could count on for audience—replace it by creating a new educated public, and being in relation to it a centre of concentration and a maintainer of standards.

With the word 'academic' of course I have implicitly recognized the scepticism that such an idea is calculated to invite among those who know the academic world. And I confess that I myself have had from time to time to fight against the sense that there is an inherent incompatibility between academic conditions and the intelligent study of literature. Standards in the sciences will always be taken care of; besides the drive of our civilization that ensures it, they lend themselves to defence and assertion immensely more. The standards proper to the field of literary study are elusive for polemical purposes in the face of scepticism and hostility. They can't be defined or demonstrated or produced, though something answering to the word and the idea can't but be postulated. To identify the problem of Higher Education in general with the problem of the university in the spirit of the Robbins report, or to countenance that identification when off one's guard, is disastrous. Of course there is a problem of Higher Education, but there can be no satisfactory solution of that problem—or of the problem of education at any level—if standards are not maintained somewhere, and they will not be maintained unless, in spite of the righteous jealousy and the automatic will to level down that present themselves in our time as democratic principle, the university is preserved—preserved for the community and the common good. And the university is the place where students working in the fields of science and mathematics, and kept aware of the standards that scientists and mathematicians can be counted on to maintain, are co-present with students whose work is in a field of literary studies where standards prevail that can be called equivalent.

I say 'literary studies' (meaning English), not because I think none of the others coming under the head of the Humanities matters: my concern for English as a liaison centre, I hope, makes that plain. The reason may be put simply by invoking the truism that English is at the other extreme from mathematics, so that the relevant standards, those with which literary criticism is con-concerned, are peculiarly difficult to keep effectively present and to defend against the drift and drive of our age, and by adding that when one examines the nature of the difficulty one is contemplating their crucial importance to civilization. I am of course meaning to recall what I said about the nature of critical standards earlier.

Well then, I know that the demand I make of English, the role I think properly assigned to it in the modern university, is such as to provoke a good deal of scepticism. And when I proceed to the considerations that bring out the cogency of the assignment, I shall invite, I know, some more scepticism. But I ask the sceptics to contemplate—to look well in the face—what their scepticism implies. When, then, I try to suggest the ways in which the role I have defined as that of the university English School could be justified, one of my assumptions is that no one will be reading English who hasn't a bent for literary study and isn't positively intelligent. To put it another way, no one should be reading English who can't benefit by 'teaching' addressed to the top level. I see the word 'teaching' in inverted commas; I don't like it, because of the suggestion it carries of telling—authoritative telling. The peculiar nature of the study of English worth pursuing at university level entails its being in the most essential regards, though a special study, not what 'specialist' suggests. A genuine teacher doesn't find himself holding back his subtlest insight and his most adventurous thought because they are not suitable for communication to first- or second-year men. He tests and develops in 'teaching' his perceptions, his understanding and his thought, and with good men may do so very fruitfully. For what we call teaching is, if genuine, a matter of enlisting and fostering collaboration; the teacher in English has, in what I have pointed to with the distinction between 'special' and 'specialist', a peculiar advantage—or a given kind of advantage in a peculiarly rewarding form. The qualifications of a teacher are given in these observations. He is one who has the kinds of interest in literature that go with finding pleasure and profit in discussing it with intelligent young students.

The educational problem, the problem of justifying an English School as a centre of higher education, looks hopeless if it is thought of in terms merely of syllabus and a standard student-product to be turned out. The undergraduate as student not only needs much contact with the kind of senior I have described; he needs to feel, and feel with good reason, that in the matter of his work and its significance he belongs to a community that is implicitly collaborative. What's in question is not merely the stimulus and help of habitual and varied intellectual intercourse; it's the sense of the field of his work as opening to him, for a developing comprehension, something real, living and of moment. In what ways the informal intellectual intercourse that is the essential for him should be promoted by a use of the discussion-method in connexion with formal studies—that is hardly a matter for general pronouncement: everyone knows that something worth doing has from time to time been done, and that the undergraduate, looking for the necessary supplement to the weekly essay-supervision, won't as a rule report that his need is met by the lecture list.

The kind of insistence I am intending in all this is, I think, plain. It is one with my stiffness about the use of the word 'university'. What's in a name?—in our age the menace, clearly, of irreversible disaster. It is an age in which we hear of a University of the Air, and in which it wouldn't be altogether gratuitous to fear that a minis-terial potentate in charge of culture may think it pro-gressive to empower an exalted and subsidized corres-pondence college to confer degrees.[1] There is good reason today for insisting that a university education is more than a matter of being lectured at, taking notes, doing a canny reading course, having some exercises marked, and being examined.

I have in any case to deal with possible scepticism about what may reasonably be expected of a university student, and the consideration I have emphasized is very much to the point. I believe that the undergraduate reading English should be treated, and treatable, as an adult. I believe that he must inevitably be faced with more than he can get properly done, and that the profit of his education will involve his realizing this in a positive way—that is, responding constructively to the situa-

[1] Since I spoke this we have had the ministerial announcement of The Open University.

tion. But for such a response he needs the conditions of work—the access to guidance, and the milieu that brings stimulus and the sense of collaborative activity—that I have described.

The academic in the bad sense will always be with us, whether as a mere nuisance or as an enemy, and it can take new forms. And this leads me to remark that the reasons for not fixing, as Oxford does, a hither limit to English literature is not that by abstaining we permit lectures on *Finnegans Wake* and the *Cantos*. It is that the very conception of what a literature is, and of how as a living reality it exists (in so far as it does), is at issue. The Oxford habit is the habit instilled by a classical training. Everyone knows the reasons given, the classical reasons, for seeing the Greek and Latin classics as the supremely appropriate *literae humaniores* for humane education: 'the literatures are complete'—that is, finished; 'all the rules are known'. The same habit betrays itself in the objection to recognizing the works of living writers—or works produced in a past not yet (it is felt) safely removed —as fit subjects of academic study: in this modern field, we are told, too much depends on the vagaries and pre-judices of personal taste and judgment. As if personal taste and real judgment—the hazards of self-committal— weren't entailed in a genuine approach to any literature, and as if it were not of the utmost importance that the student's sense of this truth should never be blunted, but should inform his work everywhere!

It is only from the present, out of the present, in the present, that you can approach the literature of the past. To put it in another way, it is only in the present that the past lives. But that is not as simple a proposition as it might at first seem to be. And it might, as any simple

68

proposition in this region might, carry an unfortunate suggestion: it might seem to endorse the naïve idea of the present that it is the business of an English School—and a university—to combat. Supposing that, with the phrase, 'A Period of English Literature', lodged in my mind, I had given as the subject of these lectures, 'English literature in the 1920s' (the earlier phase of the present, so to speak). Should I have confined myself to talking about what was written in the period, and devoted my time to discussing, and charting in relation to one another, Lawrence, Eliot, Joyce, Virginia Woolf, E. M. Forster, Lytton Strachey, and so on? No. Most certainly not.

A friend and university teacher, urging me to devote these lectures to the problem of English in the university to-day, added: 'when we haven't, as *you* had in the 1920s, the advantage of a lively contemporary development in literature'. He was right in his implication: in the 1920s, when the English Tripos was establishing itself, those working out (arduously if unofficially) the lines on which the study of literature might become the modern central humanity so much needed had an advantage over their successors who face the problem now. The 1920s were a creative period: something new and important, we could see (however little encouraged by the institutional world), was happening in English literature, and the fact of impressive new creation that compelled an intense critical interest told immensely in the war against the academic spirit—the war it made inevitable. Not only that; a serious interest in the poetic innovations entailed, in an endlessly rewarding way, a study of the relation of the present to the past that was at once new light thrown on the past and on the present. Any effective response to such prompting as came from my friend—any answer to the question: 'What do we do in a present that is not strikingly creative?'—could only take the form of suggestive illustration, given with some particularity.

I define here the spirit of what I shall be saying: 'This is how I should try to manage one of our openings, and these are the kinds of development I should hope and work for'. Of course, I shall be following the promptings of my own perception and judgment. But nothing could be less in the spirit of laying down the law, and I shan't even be doing anything like dictating a syllabus. I shall, in fact, be discussing—continuing to discuss— the theme of English literature in our time in the way that seems to me most called for, seeing that our time is what it is and that there is a university audience in front of me.

To proceed then. T. S. Eliot is not remote from us. His time—he died only the other day—is the immediate past of our present. The changes during his time, the changes since his latest creative work (which I think his most significant and impressive), serve only to sharpen our sense of his significance. And there is the further great advantage that he can't but evoke in any intelligently appreciative reader a great deal of critical dissent and adverse or qualifying or questioning commentary.

A phrase of his that gives me an opening of the kind I want for my present purpose of exemplification has been a theme for a good deal of controversial discussion; it is: 'dissociation of sensibility'. It comes from Eliot the distinguished mind, and the cluster of essays with which it associates represents that part of his criticism which makes his critical achievement momentous. And I have to add that the phrase and the context don't seem to me to have received very much intelligent attention. That amounts (at any rate for me) to saying that the achievement—that Eliot's best criticism—should be found to be worth much more to us in the field of university English, the study of English literature and of the history of English civilization, than has been generally appreciated.

What is in question, then, is (i) a just recognition of the essential and pregnant felicity of the critical constatation that Eliot focuses in the phrase, 'dissociation of sensibility'; (ii) what that entails, a keener sense—one only to be got in intelligent literary study—of the profound change in civilization that took place in the 17th century; (iii) an enlivening apprehension of the literary history, from Donne to Eliot's day, that is involved; (iv) a sharpened realization that the intelligence and insight that made Eliot so decisive in critical comment on the 17th century are inseparable from his greatness as a twentieth-century poet. I might have continued with a five, a six and a seven—and further. But they can be left to come out by the way: immediately, I will remind you of the context of Eliot's phrase, by reading (with excisions) a passage from his essay, 'The Metaphysical Poets'.

After what seems to me an unfortunate quotation from Chapman (which, I remember, was also used by Herbert Read), and an apt comparison between Lord Herbert of Cherbury and Tennyson, Eliot goes on:

> The difference is not a simple difference of degree between poets. It is something that had happened to the mind of England between the time of Donne or Lord Herbert of Cherbury and the time of Tennyson and Browning: it is the difference between the intellectual poet and the reflective

poet. ... When a poet's mind is perfectly equipped for its work, it is constantly amalgamating disparate experience; the ordinary man's experience is chaotic, irregular, fragmentary. The latter falls in love, or reads Spinoza, and these two experiences have nothing to do with each other, or with the noise of the typewriter or the smell of the cooking; in the mind of the poet these experiences are always forming new wholes.

We may express the difference by the following theory. The poets of the 17th century, the successors of the dramatists of the sixteenth, possessed a mechanism of sensibility which could devour any kind of experience. ... In the seventeenth century a dissociation of sensibility set in from which we have never recovered, and this dissociation, as is natural, was aggravated by the influence of the two most powerful poets of the century, Milton and Dryden. Each of these men performed certain poetic functions so magnificently well that the magnitude of the effect concealed the absence of others. ...

After this brief exposition of a theory ... we may ask, what would have been the fate of the 'metaphysical' had the current of poetry descended in a direct line from them, as it descended in a direct line to them? They would not certainly have been classified as metaphysical. The possible interests of a poet are unlimited; the more intelligent he is the more likely that he will have interests: our only condition is that he turn them into poetry, and not merely meditate on them poetically. ... The poets in question have, like other poets, various faults. But they were, at best, engaged in the task of trying to find the verbal equivalent for states of mind and feeling. And this means both that they are more mature, and that they wear better, than later poets of certainly not less literary ability.

I have not intended to suggest that one should read this, or ever should have read it, with unqualified acquiescence. But, as I have implied, one's indebtedness to an author by whom one has especially profited may very well be in part—in large part—a matter of the way in which he compels one to discover just how, in this and that, one disagrees, or sees a need to question. When, however, I say that Eliot's phrase, 'this brief exposition of a theory', does not strike me as a felicity it is because 'theory' seems a poor and misleading word for the critical service he has done us, or (shall I say?) did us in my time; which was to make us see certain essential facts in significant relation. No one, I suppose, will dispute that the 17th century witnessed an immense, comprehensive and momentous change in ethos, in civilization, in the English language. What Eliot does in the essays that provide the context for his phrase (which seems to me as apt and acceptable as any that could be found) is to suggest, compellingly and with sufficient precision to be unanswerable, how the change is focused in the changing use of the English language in poetry—and poetry, remember, mattered in the 17th century, mattered in a way it is hard to realize fully now.

When I say 'unanswerable' I am not forgetting that offers have been made to controvert Eliot's judgments and suggestions, to expose his confusions and imprecisions and fallacies, and to dismiss ironically those of us who have found him, in this part of his criticism, decisively illuminating and in essence incontrovertible. An example you can easily turn up is to be found in J. B. Leishman's book on Donne, *The Monarch of Wit* (page 87, and on for some twenty pages). It may fairly be called representative; I don't think any that is more creditable as an offer of critical intelligence can be produced. And I pick on the book because it is a useful one and worth both seriousness and severity of attention. It would be profitable to go through those pages, making the appropriate commentary.

F

I myself shan't do that, though I will comment on an opening passage by way of enforcing the point (it should be obvious enough) that Leishman's kind of poised confidence in his qualifications—that of an Oxford scholar who has translated Rilke and collaborated with a modern poet in doing it, makes it impossible for him to try and understand what a critic, a real and supremely original one, is saying—or doing. The point is an important one for those of us who believe that the survival of literature in our civilization depends very largely on the possibility of intelligent literary study at universities.

Consider this, then—Leishman has just made his initial concession (one that would not have been made by a scholar-critic in the 1920s) that Eliot's critical writings 'contain much that is illuminating and much that is true':

'Nevertheless, these essays also contain much that is either demonstrably untrue, or true only to a very limited extent and after having been subjected to very great qualifications. They were, in fact, written under certain limitations which the author nowhere admits and of which only a few of his readers can be aware. In the first place, it is difficult'—for a real scholar and specialist, let me interject—'not to suppose that Mr Eliot's knowledge of so-called metaphysical poetry did not at that time extend very much further than Sir Herbert Grierson's anthology, and that his high estimate of it and his readiness to praise it at the expense of other kinds of English poetry were partly determined by the fact that he knew it only at its best.'

The assumptions carried here on the calm assurance are beautifully betraying, the mode of argument so blindly beside the point and its intention so gratuitous.

Even if Eliot's knowledge of the metaphysicals had been as restricted as the authority insinuates, the essay itself shows that Eliot knew enough for his purpose. For his purpose, it was metaphysical poetry at its best that he needed to know; the worst, of which he was far from showing the ignorance that Leishman imputes, was irrelevant. What the scholar cannot admit—and 'cannot' seems the right word—is the purpose.

The purpose is of the kind of which the student of literature needs to cultivate the most inward understanding; inward, sympathetic and active. Without such a preoccupation he may acquire what passes for knowledge, but it will be pretty worthless, and not of a kind an English School should foster or reward. I remember that, in the 1920s, a pupil of mine said to a senior of great reputation and distinguished acquaintance in the literary world: 'What we want, to deal with that problem, is someone with Eliot's combination of knowledge and critical insight'. 'Oh Tom doesn't know as much as you think', came the reply; 'he's very clever; he makes a little go a long way'. 'It's a pity', retorted my pupil, who came from Lancashire, 'it's a pity, Dr X, there aren't a few more merely clever people who can make as little go as far'.

It's true, of course, that the earlier Eliot sometimes makes himself suspect of wanting to impress. But in his best criticism—and especially in the essays that Leishman picks on for animadversion—he does with the mastery of genius what we all in any serious study of English literature are trying to do. That is why his critical work on the 17th century is worth close attention. The specific insights he communicates are of immense value—to say which is not to suggest that they can be just taken over as if they were a kind of certified factual knowledge. The very qualities that provoke Leishman to distaste and superiority when he has the essay on the 'metaphysicals' in front of him make this plain, for they make mere inert taking-over impossible. In the reader who truly reads it (and Leishman doesn't) the essay compels a response that is both energetically constructive *and* critical, as well as being selective in different ways at different times. That is, it is criticism of the highest order: pregnant, intensely economical, and, in the way of great criticism, unmistakably creative, it exemplifies with classical force the essentially collaborative spirit of critical judgment—the real and therefore personal judgment that has the implicit form I suggested.

This best criticism of Eliot's properly receives the emphasis in any attempt to suggest on what lines, and in what spirit, an intelligent study of English literature (which is a large and complex field) will be pursued at the university. Leishman supplies a relevant provocation to make some points when he continues:

> In the second place, both in these essays and elsewhere, Mr Eliot was writing not merely in a spirit of disinterested curiosity but (though he never explicitly admits it) with something of an axe to grind. He was writing, not merely as a critic, but as a poet, as what he himself calls a 'poetic practitioner', and a question always at the back of his mind was this: 'From what earlier poets can a modern English poet most profitably learn?' His preoccupation with this question largely explains both his exaltation of the so-called metaphysical poets and that denigration of Milton which he continued intermittently for the next twenty years.

What Leishman means by a 'spirit of disinterested curiosity' he makes plain enough, and Eliot, being in his best and decisive criticism a great critic, most certainly doesn't write in that spirit. The disinterestedness of a critic—a real one—is something quite different. It expresses an intense interest in life, and life, there is point in saying in such a context as this, is here and now. It is only in the present that even the literature of the past—and the 'even' is unnecessary—can live. It follows that 'English literature'—I put the phrase in inverted commas, but I know that it portends the most important of realities—will, so long as it *is* a living and effective reality, change from age to age in a way that is more disturbing to scholars than mere accretion. Of course, the change associated with Eliot's name took a critic of genius to bring it about, and without being that he couldn't have been the poet he was. But every student of literature is a critic, at least in aspiration, or else he is merely wasting his time. And one of the things that a student who was modestly but in a real way a critic would have been doing forty or thirty or even fewer years ago was helping to get the significance of Eliot's criticism—that is, of his critical and creative work in association—recognized.

My last parenthesis, like Leishman's charge, points to the peculiar critical felicity of what he calls Eliot's 'axe to grind'. This, which Leishman treats as regrettable —or, rather, as an opportunity for the fully equipped scholar to show his superiority as a guide, is Eliot's supreme qualification, that which made him so decisive a critic. The 'question always at the back of his mind' (and it surely took no divination to arrive at Leishman's account of it) was an intense particular kind of interest that, his genius being what it was, enabled him to give, in taking the opportunities presented by a book for review and a tercentenary address to be delivered, what amounts in effect to a quintessential history of English poetry—one both revolutionary and compelling. And as a man reading English should be encouraged and helped to perceive for himself, more than poetry is involved.

I say 'amounts in effect': the essays are marvels of pregnancy. Only a mind directed and charged in the way that Leishman deprecates could have produced them. And they are products of the true disinterestedness, that which is a necessary virtue in both critics and creative writers. What Leishman calls an 'axe to grind' ensured the disinterestedness—the strong relevant play of undeflected intelligence. Eliot says of certain minor poets of the 18th century that 'they had not the consciousness to perceive that they felt differently and therefore must use words differently' from what the established conventions dictated. He is implicitly recording here the obvious enough truth that his own creative achievement of demonstrating that something could happen in English poetry after Swinburne had entailed the feat of critical intelligence represented by these most important essays.

They contain a highly compressed charge of perceptions, intuitions and suggestions. They offer no simple diagnostic formulas and no simple prescriptions, and I should have thought that they make that plain. They need to be read as what they are (criticism, but—or and—an important part of the creative writing of our time), and not as what a scholar insists they must be. Complex, packed and delicately organized, they obviously don't present an expository development of any one thematic strand, and so do obviously count on an energy of active critical intelligence in the reader—

intelligence that responds constructively as well as in the questioning or dissenting way that is commonly felt to be meant by 'critically'. A critical element in the form of questioning or dissent, at this point and that, there will be in any intelligent response. To say this is to note one of the essential qualifications of Eliot's criticism for the use I would assign to it. There is nothing of the dogmatically prescriptive about it; its authority is a matter of that in it which compels a recognition of its rightness.

There has been more formidable criticism than Leishman's of the passages that form the immediate context of 'dissociation of sensibility'. We printed thirty years ago in *Scrutiny* James Smith's essay on 'Metaphysical Poetry'[1], in which he comments severely on Eliot's talk about 'felt thought' and on such formulations as 'a thought to him was an experience; it modified his sensibility'. That essay repays attention, but it doesn't, I think, seriously damage the criticized essay as the effective expression of Eliot's directing interest and aim. I do indeed think that the censured formulations represent a deep-seated preoccupation of his, one that turns out to be essential in what I take to be his distinctive creative achievement; for in a unique and astonishing way he developed a poetic of an intense intellectual interest; he made poetry the means and the communication of profound original thought. But the kind of emphasis the theme of 'metaphysical' poetry gets in his essay is an accident of that occasion (Grierson's anthology for review) which Eliot had turned into an opportunity, and it is a little confusing. Eliot himself implicitly recognizes

[1] Reprinted in *A Selection from Scrutiny*. Vol. II (Cambridge University Press).

this, and provides the corrective, here—I'll read the sentences again:

'we must ask, what would have been the fate of the "metaphysical" had the current of poetry descended in a direct line from them, as it descended in a direct line to them? They would not, certainly, be classified as metaphysical. The possible interests of a poet are un-limited; the more intelligent he is the better, and the more intelligent, the more likely to have interests: our only condition is that he turn them into poetry, and not merely meditate on them poetically.'

There, in that last sentence, the essential thing is said. With a view to bringing out its force, and vindicating the intention, spirit and efficacy of the criticism that gives 'dissociation of sensibility' its context, I would remind you of an early poem of Eliot's, 'Portrait of a Lady', which appeared in *Prufrock* (1917). It is characteristic of the peculiar genius to which we are indebted that the creative work of the decisively modern poet should, while giving edge to the critic's meaning, further the illumination of the past effected by his seventeenth-century commentaries.

As I remarked in a recent attempt at a characterization of Eliot's total creative achievement (now that there was no more to come from him), one ought to have been struck enough by 'Portrait of a Lady' and 'The Love Song of J. Alfred Prufrock', reading them in the early nineteen-twenties, to say: 'But already in 1917 this young poet had effectively 'altered expression'. One couldn't, of course, have said just that, since Eliot's dictum—'Sensibility alters in us all from age to age whether we will or no, but expression is only altered by a man of genius'—wasn't published till 1930. But one ought, confronted with those poems, to have been able to recognize an achievement of a kind the dictum defines, and to have said: 'At last it's demonstrated that something *can* happen after Swinburne'. One couldn't, though, have said just that—even that; one didn't know until Eliot made one realize it that there had been a Swinburnian arrest, that Swinburne had been a dead-end. It's a classical illustration (or should be), one close and accessible to us, of the way in which a climate of assumptions and habits of which we are unconscious determines our awareness—or our unawareness. 'They had not the consciousness to perceive that they felt differently and therefore must use words differently.' The force of this proposition in its bearing on Eliot's achievement is something that Leishman, though a scholar in the seventeenth century and conscious of being a modern critic too, couldn't take.

There is nothing in 'Portrait of a Lady' that suggests Donne, or Jacobean dramatic verse, or any 'metaphysical'. Nor is there anything that suggests Jules Laforgue (I am recalling Eliot's statement to the effect that his starting-places are to be found in certain French poets of the 19th century and certain sixteenth-century dramatists). Nevertheless, as a study of his verse up to and including 'The Waste Land' will bring out very clearly, his statement was well-founded; it suggests a critically illuminating account of his actual way to the achieved new poetic of 'Portrait of a Lady'.

The versification and language of that poem are wholly of the twentieth century and wholly without suggestion of archaism or pastiche or reminiscence. The rhythms and metric are such that no one brought up on Victorian poetry could have had any difficulty in recognizing them as proper to verse. What was disconcerting was the play of tone and inflection, and that is what takes us to the astonishing newness, the innovation, the originality.

Such a play of tone and inflection is something you don't find in Victorian poetry, or Georgian.

> *I take my hat: how can I make a cowardly amends*
> *For what she has said to me*
> *You will see me any morning in the park*
> *Reading the comics and the sporting page.*
> *Particularly I remark*
> *An English countess goes upon the stage.*
> *A Greek was murdered at a Polish dance,*
> *Another bank defaulter has confessed.*
> *I keep my countenance,*
> *I remain self-possessed*
> *Except when a street piano, mechanical and tired*
> *Reiterates some worn-out common song*
> *With the smell of hyacinths across the garden*
> *Recalling things that other people have desired.*
> *Are these ideas right or wrong*

This doesn't suggest Donne, or any other seventeenth-century poet—or any intense intellectuality. But actually the play of tone and inflection mean the possibility of a kind of strong and subtle thinking in poetry, an intellectual nerve, that explains Eliot's interest in the metaphysicals.

III
Eliot's 'Axe to Grind', and the Nature of Great Criticism

ELIOT'S 'AXE TO GRIND',
AND THE NATURE OF
GREAT CRITICISM

I KNOW, of course, that 'sensibility' is a tricky word,
one difficult to define for our purposes. But it is not for
that any less an essential word. It can't, I think, be so
fixed by definition as not to shift in force as we use it—
as we find ourselves having to use it. But that is a peculi-
arity of important words—words we find we can't do
without—in the field of our distinctive discipline of
intelligence (for, I repeat, we ought to think of the
distinctive discipline of literary study as that, and be able
to justify the attitude). What the critic has to do is to
cultivate a vigilant responsibility, so that the shifts
confuse or mislead neither the reader nor himself. And
'sensibility' is a word to which the student ought to
give a great deal of thoughtful attention; new perceptions and realizations are likely to result. There can hardly
be a better text for bringing that home to him and
starting fruitful discussion than this central, this pre-
eminently focal, criticism of Eliot's.

Eliot's essential criteria or desiderata and his positive
concern, I mean those which he invokes when he talks
about the 'dissociation of sensibility', are given (let me
read the sentence once again) here: 'The possible interests
of a poet are unlimited; the more intelligent he is, the
better; the more intelligent he is the more likely to have
interests: our only condition is that he turn them into
poetry, and not merely meditate on them poetically'.
What Eliot wants as the climate of assumptions and

habits in which the poet works, and the tradition of technique and expressive convention in which the assumptions insinuate their hold on the poet, so determining his approach, are indicated there plainly enough. The formulation is distinctively of our time; that is, post-1914. That we can say that, is due to Eliot. It was he who made us realize that for the greater part of a century formal poetry, in relation to the novel (he didn't put it in this way, nor did it occur to him to do so—a point to which I shall revert), had ceased to matter. In the post-Romantic period the creative strength of the English language—the poetic strength—had gone into prose fiction.

The significance of this development, the history behind it and the consequences in twentieth-century literature, challenge the literary student to an inquiry of key importance for an intelligent grasp of English literary history. The criticism of Eliot's I am examining, and of which the scholars and academic critics in general have made so little, offers, in its pregnancy (a matter of the significant concentration that goes with the 'axe to grind' and focuses an immense fund and force of suggestion), an incomparable opening into such an inquiry. That is why the student should be incited and helped to make the most of it. For what, faced with the vast wildernesses of reading he is supposed to tackle, he desperately needs is the means—which may be described as the energy of an intelligent confidence that derives from some sound guiding and organizing perceptions and insights—of starting to develop for himself a grasp of an inclusive field of English literature in terms of significant relations between its parts. The suggested use of Eliot would promote the antithesis of the kind of

play with ideas, categories and 'explanations' that, in the
past century, has produced, in one guise or another,
pseudo-scientific or 'social', so much irrelevance offered
as literary history and so much abstract gratuitousness
as critical enlightenment. For Eliot's best criticism is
that of the poet who 'altered expression' round about
1920; it starts from the specificities of poetry in the
concrete and always takes the reader back to them.

And a further point is that, when one ponders it, it
brings home to one with peculiar vividness the nature
of a living relation between the past and the present, and
the force of the truth that it is in the present that the past
has its life. What gives Eliot his acuteness as a critic of
poetry and poetic development in the seventeenth century
is his diagnostic (and creative) concern with the state of
things in 1920. But having said that I draw back, feeling
bound to say correctively that his interest in the seventeenth century had most certainly a great deal to do with
his acuteness about his own time, and about his poetic
problems as problems of his own time. His early poetry,
with its clear indebtedness to the past, shows that.

'Portrait of a Lady', from which I read last week, is
not an example; it shows in itself no clear indebtedness
to any poetry of the seventeenth century—or to any
French poets of the nineteenth, for that matter; that is
why I picked on it for my purpose. I wanted to get out
of the way Leishman's kind of misconception about the
nature and significance of Eliot's interest in Donne and
the 'metaphysicals'; also, more generally, the much too
common misconceptions about the way a great poet is
'indebted'. Free from any intellectual difficulty, or
difficulty of any kind, as 'Portrait of a Lady' is, un-
aggressive as is the originality of its versification, it

shows the poet's portentous new mastery in its supple, sensitive and daring play of tone and inflexion. 'He seems capable', one might have said, 'of demonstrating in due course his command of a poetic that need exclude from poetry none of the interests of a cultivated person alive in the twentieth century.' One might also have said of the poem: 'It suggests that poetry might have something of the fulness and freedom of access to experience —all the elements of experience—that we associate with the work of a distinguished novelist'.

If we are asked to explain what the poem can have owed to Eliot's studies in the seventeenth century, we have the clue to the answer in the matter-of-fact way in which, at the end of a sentence, he refers to the 'metaphysicals' as the 'successors of the dramatists'. To bring out the justice and force of such a reference we have only to look at Donne's couplets in the 'rough' mode (it has been something of a habit to call it that) of the satires:

> *Are not heavens joyes as valiant to assuage*
> *Lusts, as earth's honour was to them? Alas,*
> *As wee do them in meanes, shall they surpasse*
> *Us in the end, and shall thy father's spirit*
> *Meet blinde Philosophers in heaven, whose merit*
> *Of strict life may be imputed faith, and heare*
> *Thee, whom hee taught so easie wayes and neare*
> *To follow, damn'd? O if thou dar'st, feare this . . .*

As I've said, they are couplets. But, though the rime is positively used, the rhythmic ethos of the versification —a matter of the way in which Donne uses the spoken language and the speaking voice—makes us think of Shakespearean blank-verse. The play of the sense-movement across the verse-structure that produces the delayed

88

and dramatic stress on 'damn'd' is decidedly Shakespearean. And in

> *Are not heavens joyes as valiant to assuage*
> *Lusts*

the rime, which insists on the line-division, serves to
reinforce the familiar Shakespearean use of the run-over
that gives that sardonic deliberateness to 'lusts'.

Donne in 'Satyre III' is unmistakably a 'successor of
the dramatists'—or of Shakespeare, we may surely say;
Shakespeare who after all was *the* dramatist. But there is
no difference relevant to the given point between Donne's
satire and his lyrics or non-satiric poems.

> *I wonder by my troth, what thou, and I*
> *Did, till we lov'd*

—responding to such effects, and considering Donne's
so characteristic poetic, I again and again find passages
of Eliot coming into my mind:

> *Under a juniper-tree the bones sang scattered and*
> * shining*
> *We are glad to be scattered, we did little good to each*
> * other*
> *Under a tree in the cool of the day, with the blessing of*
> * sand,*
> *Forgetting themselves and each other, united*
> *In the quiet of the desert. This is the land which ye*
> *Shall divide by lot. And neither division nor unity*
> *Matters. This is the land. We have our inheritance.*

Eliot's rhythm and resonance are intensely his own,
but that juxtaposition is surely suggestive enough in the
sense I have intimated. And indeed I needn't say much
more about the nature of Eliot's interest in Donne, and
the misleadingness of laying the emphasis on what he

G   89

says about 'felt thought' in that essay on Grierson's anthology. One oughtn't to find oneself generalizing easily about Eliot's style, for it presents great variety. But even in *Ash-Wednesday*, as the brief quotation I have just made illustrates, the style, for all its liturgical suggestion, remains in touch with those styles of his which most obviously bear out his hint about his indebtedness to dramatic verse. It has no tendency to the hypnoidal; on the contrary, it challenges constantly the closest and fullest waking attention, the most acutely perceptive, the most delicately discriminating, responsiveness. This is true of Eliot's poetry in all its phases, and in saying this I indicate the sense in which *Four Quartets*, though a surprising development out of 'Portrait of a Lady', is not, after all, a paradoxical one. And though Eliot's interest in Donne was of a different nature from that exemplified in the half-dozen poems of William Empson's that appeared in *Cambridge Poetry* 1929 (they were very impressive), Eliot was far from uninterested in the ways in which Donne's poetry expressed a strong addiction to 'thought'.

The potentiality of intellectual strength is there in that early mode of Eliot's, which, as I have said, doesn't make one think of Donne, though an essential relation to Donne stares at one when one reads 'Satyre III' and ponders Eliot's reference to the 'metaphysicals' as the 'successors of the dramatists'. And that reference is a cue for noting that the capacity for intellectual strength as Eliot postulates it is something that goes with a command of concreteness, manifested in sensuous strength and a charged and complex life of imagery. And the upshot is, surely, that there is more to be said than it has always seemed easy to grant even for formulations in that essay that have most invited irony. I suppose that I myself have not chosen since (say) 1930 to quote the passage about reading Spinoza, falling in love, the smell of the cooking and the sound of the typewriter. But the advantage of reading a respectable example of poised and deprecatory academic comment is that one is provoked to tell oneself that Eliot wrote in a particular situation at a particular time and under journalistic conditions—he took the opportunity; and took it in a way that after all produced a classical and decisive piece of criticism. One asks then, rhetorically (for the answer is plain): How could it have been done better? What better than the effective and final can one ask for? It came in the only way it could have come—as it couldn't have come from a consciously poised and judicious scholar with no 'axe to grind'.

About the causes of the process of 'dissociation' Eliot says very little. He is aware (as who is not?) that civilization underwent something like a total change in the seventeenth century, and he concerns himself with what seem to him the important manifestations of the change as they appear in English poetry. Of these he shows himself a supremely acute judge and analyst; and in his necessarily short essays, the effect of which depends on their concentrated impact, there is no scope for what would require a treatise, nor is it *his* business (and he has no doubts about what that should be) to write one: his approach is the poet's of 1920. To undertake what, implicitly, he prompts us to—some relating of literary change to the seventeenth-century transformations of the human world—is *our* business. Of course, in spite of my parenthetic 'as who is not?', the ironic superiority with which Eliot's 'dissociation' has been dismissed betrays a failure to be aware, an inability to think, of the revolutionary change in civilization as having a possible relevance to such an issue, which is one of poetic convention and use.

Confronted, then, with the poised innocence that treats Eliot's phrase as gratuitous and absurd, one can point to what Dryden did with *Antony and Cleopatra*. That is a good tactical move, the expectation being that one will resort to what Leishman calls Eliot's 'denigration of Milton'. Eliot doesn't denigrate Milton; he merely, in a minimal way, characterizes him; or, rather, reminds us of certain Miltonic peculiarities. These peculiarities are important, and Milton, in English history, is of transcendent importance. But it wasn't his genius to be representative in the way Dryden is, and moreover, the question of Milton's part in the 'dissociation of sensibility' is bedevilled by militant piety as Dryden's isn't. Though an accomplished academic may still find it natural to speak of Dryden's 'proud and lovely masterpiece', and you will not surprise or displease anyone who matters if you say that *All For Love* is a better play than *Antony and Cleopatra*, no one is touchy about Dryden.

What he did to the intensely Shakespearean work he did with satisfaction, confidence and—for all his sincere tribute to Shakespeare's superior genius—a certain modest unawareness of what he was doing. If he *had* been aware he couldn't have done it; his confidence was that of the brilliant writer who knows he has the world with him, who feels himself to be the voice of the new triumphant spirit of civilization, and who is sure of acclaim from the recognized 'best contemporary taste'. And what he did to Shakespeare is given in the difference between his rendering of 'The barge she sat in' and the original speech (Enobarbus's). He eliminated the concreteness, and for the poetry—the exquisitely sensitive dramatic poetry—substituted eloquence (*Prends l'éloquence et tord lui le cou*). The marvel of evoked and re-enacted life he replaced by noble statement, and the living diversity by a uniform elocutionary decorum. As I brought out (not a difficult business) in an analytic comparison I once made,[1] the infinitely various Shakespearean imagery is in *All for Love* reduced to illustrative simile; the prose-idea has come first and the work of the image is to present it poetically. Metaphor is simile with the 'like' or 'as' left out, and simile, when sustained, is lucid, uncomplicated and uncompressed; a matter of simple point-by-point comparison, illustrative and obvious, the felicity residing in the obviousness (which, in our sense of it, we can hardly separate from the declamatory eloquence with which the statement is made).

No one will dispute that Dryden has a peculiarly representative quality in relation to his age. In blank verse (to adopt, adapt and re-apply a phrase of Eliot's) he stands as the Chinese wall between Shakespeare and the first age of bardolatry. An intimately related observation is that the eighteenth century, in its sustained aspiration to produce poetic tragedy, could only demonstrate its inherent incapacity for the tragic. A further observation immediately to the point is that Dryden's hey-day was the time when a modern English prose was first established; that is, when England achieved and put into general use the norms of a prose of common currency —lucid, logical, business-like and idiomatic. When we

[1] See *Scrutiny*, Vol. V. ' "Antony and Cleopatra" and "All for Love": a Critical Exercise'.

ask how it was that modern prose appeared so decisively in the first decade of the Restoration, with an effect of having prevailed over-night, the answer is an account of the total movement of civilization that then, after twenty years of civil war and Commonwealth, made itself felt as the decisive start of a new age, and the sure promise of triumphant human achievement. A modern prose, the product of the conditions—something like a new civilization—represented by the new status of London, was there when the Court came back, and the Restoration gave it the endorsement of the characteristic positive ethos that so rapidly defined itself and established its dominance. With the Restoration came the Royal Society. Sprat's *History of the Royal Society* belongs to 1667, and it contains a well-known passage describing the kind of prose the Society required of its members. It exacted, he says, 'a close, naked, natural way of speaking—positive expression, clear senses, a native easiness, bringing all things as near the mathematical plainness as they can, and preferring the language of artisans, countrymen and merchants before that of wits and scholars.'

What is significant about this passage is the way in which it testifies to the nature and strength of the new ethos. Sprat seems unaware of any shift of criterion when he passes from 'close' and 'naked' to 'natural', or from 'positive expressions' and 'clear senses' to 'a native easiness' and back again to 'bringing all things as near the mathematical plainness as they can', and he clearly finds a perfect naturalness in his transition to the phrase about 'the language of artisans, countrymen and merchants'. The intellectual and methodological ideals associated with the Royal Society and the great name of

Newton consort, as if belonging to the same realm, with criteria of polite manners, commonsense and social reasonableness. This is the age of Locke and the Glorious Revolution, and of Dryden, the great poet who showed what it was to be 'correct' (and what does 'correct' mean?).

All the forces of change that had been at work through the century had come together to inaugurate the triumphant advance towards the civilization, technological and Benthamite, that we live in. It isn't necessary, and it wouldn't be good economy for me, in my limited time, to make any show of holding forth on this theme. But the student ought to know—this point at least I must make—that it's *his* business to see (duly aided) that *he* is able to hold forth on it, intelligently and knowledgeably. His advisers and guides, acquitting themselves of their responsibility in the matter of reading suggestions and whatever other help can be contrived, would have done such consulting and enlisting of qualified colleagues in the various departments as they had found possible. This is an essential way in which the liaison function I have postulated will take effect. Such an account may not sound impressive; but a little real liaison—a little genuine collaborative contact between specialist studies and English—at the senior level, has a disproportionate importance: statistical measures and arguments, in the order of thought and calculation that concerns us, haven't the place they must, it seems, have in the report of a Prime Minister's committee of inquiry. And this truth applies when we ask what, at the student level, is the profit to be hoped for. The extra-literary knowledge the student whose main study is English literature acquires may, to the specialist in each field, look negligible, but it will be part of a human meaning—it will have contributed to the creation of a human meaning. The nature of literary study, properly conceived, ensures that; it compels a continually fresh realization of the nature of the third realm, and of the way in which meaning belongs there.

Educational reform as conceived by Lord Snow (I take him as representative—merely that) can only play a part in destroying education. The idea of making science students attend lectures on English literature and students in the humanities attend lectures on science is pitiful in its futility. It can effect nothing real, and the unreal, however impressively multiplied, remains what it is. As for 'mixed courses', they must be regarded with suspicion. And when, in relation to a new university, you read of a 'new break-through' you have reason to fear the worst.

To come back to 'dissociation of sensibility': perhaps the phrase doesn't convey a perfect account of the consequences of the great seventeenth-century change for poetry. But what phrase does?—what phrase could? Eliot's seems to me to have at any rate some felicity, and no better has been proposed; merely the theme has been blandly evaded. The process noted by him in those early essays is one by which the most essential differences between the distinctively poetic use of language and the prose use are being eliminated. The criteria that justify such a summary, which is mine—not Eliot's, are those he evokes in what should be a well-known passage on Beaumont and Fletcher (it comes in the essay on Ben Jonson):

> If we look at the work of Jonson's great contemporaries, Shakespeare, and also Donne and Webster and Tourneur (and sometimes Middleton), have a depth, a third dimension

..., which Jonson's work has not. Their words have often a network of tentacular roots reaching down to the deepest terrors and desires. Jonson's most certainly have not; but in Beaumont and Fletcher we may think that at times we find it. Looking closer, we discover that the blossoms of Beaumont's and Fletcher's imagination draw no sustenance from the soil, but are cut and slightly withered flowers stuck into sand.

What in Shakespearean poetry Eliot is describing is the concrete livingness, the immediacy of sensuous and life-charged presentation, that precludes any idea of a sense abstractable for paraphrase and moved Johnson, with the 'Come, thick night!' speech of Macbeth in front of him, to testify: 'In this passage is exerted all the force of poetry, that force which calls new powers into being, which embodies sentiment, and animates matter ...'. In spite of his eighteenth-century assumptions and habits, he finds himself compelled to recognize, and to describe as such, the qualities that for us constitute the differentia of poetic presentation; he is implicitly constating the difference which we think of as the difference between *presenting* or *doing* and merely telling, between evoking the concrete and describing discursively. Johnson wouldn't have said anything of the kind about a passage of *All for Love*, or the description he so much admires in Congreve's *The Mourning Bride*.

That Eliot sees a representative significance in what he notes of Beaumont and Fletcher he makes quite plain in his further reference, which comes in another early essay, that on Massinger: 'Massinger is, in fact, at a further remove from Shakespeare than that other precursor of Milton, John Fletcher.' He has just said: 'Massinger precedes, not another Shakespeare, but Milton'.

97

The part that Eliot attributes to Milton in the 'dissociation' is defined by passing references that get their force from the total context. He assumes that the Miltonic characteristics he has in mind as immediately relevant to his theme are obvious, and ask for no more than a recalling phrase or two. I myself for my purpose need make only these points. Milton's genius is to be described not merely as *un-* but as *anti-* Shakespearean. The ethos of his stylistic invention denies his verse anything like a Shakespearean relation to the living language. With the absence of the speech-subtlety of movement, tone and inflection that can be commanded only by the poet who appeals to the reader's most delicate sense of what is natural in English speech goes a marked restriction of the part played by evoked sensuous effects and evoked specific varieties of energy—an absence, in sum, of arresting concreteness. An impressiveness of sound—sound that insists on being appreciated as such ('music')—tends to predominate in the Miltonic poetic. What it offers is eloquence. Milton is, of course, essentially and very consciously, concerned with meaning, and he conceives it as something to which his relation will be one of statement; it is something to be stated, and where necessary argued with impressive and declamatory eloquence (Eliot's word is 'magniloquence').

Of course, I know that so simple a formulation invites all kinds of questions. But my emphasis on *statement* is, I think, justified; it makes a necessary critical point. The justification is to be seen in the attraction Milton had for Dryden and in the affinity that Dryden so clearly felt, and, further, in the way in which the line of Miltonic verse accompanied the Augustan line through the eighteenth century. And, to revert to the consequence for poetry of the triumphant new ethos of Dryden's time, the point I have had in view to make is that it was the loss of any essential distinction between a poetic use of language and the prose use. The eighteenth century knew only one kind of use for language: you get your ideas clear; then, with the aid of judgment, you find *les mots justes* for them. Everything a man may need to express is provided for by the words in the dictionary, used in their defined meanings, and put together according to the laws of logic, grammar and syntax.

Eliot, in his introduction to Johnson's satires, puts it: 'so positive was the culture of that age that . . . it crushed a number of smaller men who felt differently, but did not dare to face the fact'. But the situation for potential poets was worse than that; the 'positiveness' of the culture amounted to a blank denial of creativity—creativity as an inescapable fact of life. It eliminated the creative function.

Of course, this proposition needs some qualifying. Eliot in the same essay bears his testimony to that effect, as well as—with a curious unawareness—to the major truth about the 'positive culture', when he pronounces that 'to have the virtues of good prose is the first and minimum requirement of good poetry'. Yes, there *was* memorable verse written in the Augustan tradition, and the dictum would have had felicity enough as a generalization if it had ended 'good eighteenth-century poetry', or if the context had conveyed that limitation. But the generality Eliot actually intends is indefensible.

The significance of the lapse is the restricted and merely occasional nature of his interest in the eighteenth century. With 'The Vanity of Human Wishes' at his centre of attention, he is not thinking (I doubt if he ever did) about the part played by the 'positive culture' in the genesis of the Victorian, and post-Victorian, poetic climate he had to contend against in 1920. He sees the 'prose virtues' exemplified in Johnson's poem as offering an admonitory contrast to the vagueness, and the intellectual debility, of 'soul'. He observes that 'wit', in eighteenth-century poetry accompanies the prose virtues. He might have said (and perhaps does virtually say) that the claim to poetic status depends on it. And the definition of 'wit' here that I would give is: a conscious neatness and precision of statement tending towards epigram.

A further point is made, and a very important one, when we call it 'polite wit'. The 'prose virtues' are intimately associated, as indeed is every aspect of the cultural code of the eighteenth century, with manners. The distinctive characteristics of 'politeness' stand out when we compare it with the 'urbanity' that Eliot discusses as 'wit' in the essay on Marvell. He observes there that the 'unknown quality'—'unknown', he has just said, 'to the present age'—'of which we speak is probably a literary rather than a personal quality, or, more truly, that it is a quality of a civilization, of a traditional habit of life'. He is talking of the quality that leads us to relate Marvell back by way of the Caroline courtly poets to Ben Jonson. And if it is not, so far as appreciative recognition goes, unknown to us now, that is because of the way Eliot's criticism has taken effect. We are in a position to observe how the achievement in which Eliot justly credits Jonson with a major part— the establishing of a poetic tradition that expresses a traditional habit of life—implied a relation to manners not characteristic of Jonson, though his robust genius was needed to show how English verse could have Latin qualities of ideal 'civilization' and be strongly and nervously English at the same time. Marvell's urbanity derives from the courtly poets who, with reason, paid their tributes to Jonson: it is indeed the quality of a civilization; a civilization two-centred—in the Court and the country house. In it weightier values, carrying with them a suggestion of Latin authority and dignity, make themselves felt in association with manners.

This is what in the essay on Marvell Eliot identifies with 'wit'. It is succeeded, after the great change that crystallizes at the Restoration, by the polite wit of the Augustan poets, which is very significantly different, in a way characteristic of the 'positive civilization'. The reference to manners and to the social, or public, world is a much more direct, actual and simple business. The poet is a polite writer addressing a polite reader. The diction and movement of the verse suggest with a simple and limiting directness social gesture and expression, and we don't commonly ask what 'precision' means when Eliot speaks of Goldsmith's 'melting sentiment' as 'just held in check by the precision of his language'—taxing as it would be to have to define the force of the word.

We can see (and we may take 'wit' here to cover both the urbane and the polite) that Eliot is stating the clear and simple fact when he says that 'this quality is not found in Wordsworth, Shelley or Keats' (he might have added Blake). In saying this, of course, he is merely clinching his definition: Wordsworth, Shelley and Keats are all, in their different ways, concerned to communicate experience and attitudes that aren't congenial to any ethos of manners.

But equally 'this quality' is not to be found in Eliot. How could it be? There was no 'civilization' in his world to support such a quality. It is true that the Bloomsbury of the 1920s went in for the *dix-huitième* and had produced Lytton Strachey and Clive Bell's coterie manifesto entitled *Civilization*, and that Bloomsbury (in a patronizing way) took up Eliot, who let himself *be* taken up. But that is one of the less pleasant aspects of his case and career. Whatever his own delusions (which I shall have to refer to later) about the possibility of a triumphant alliance between his creative genius and his weakness for the social world, he can hardly have imagined a discussible modern poet producing, or trying to produce, a mode analogous to Marvell's 'urbanity' or 'wit'.

What was the relevance then, to his own problem of his interest in it? There is, of course, no difficulty at all in finding an answer. We are prompted to one by the comparison he makes between Marvell's 'The Nymph and the Fawn' and Morris's *I know a little garden close*. He points out that if you want to compare Morris's poem with one of Marvell's, it can't be with 'The Coy Mistress' (also about love and death): that would be too silly. It will have to be with 'The Nymph and the Fawn'; and then, though Marvell's poem offers frankly a playful lightness, it is seen to be in an important sense the more serious of the two. It knows just what it is; the assurance is there in the poise of what Eliot calls the wit, of which he says at the end of the essay on Marvell: 'It involves, probably, a recognition implicit in the expression of every experience, of other kinds of experience which are possible, which we find as clearly in the greatest as in poets like Marvell'. He has said just before: 'it is confused with cynicism because it implies a constant inspection and criticism of experience'. That is, it implies that the poet appeals to the full waking and thinking mind

of the reader. There we have the obvious relevance of
Eliot's interest in it to the creative problem facing the
'practitioner' of 1920. But he covers too much with the
word 'urbanity', so that his use of it involves an emphasis
that misleads and confuses. Of the qualities the Marvell
essay brings under the term, those that mattered to the
'practitioner' are those which in 'The Metaphysical
Poets' he attributes to Donne and his school and to the
dramatists who can be seen as the pupils of Shakespeare;
and to Donne and Shakespeare, who so obviously
mattered more to the poet of 'Gerontion', *The Waste
Land* and 'Marina' than Marvell did, he explicitly does
not attribute urbanity. It is for the inquirer into the
'dissociation of sensibility' to compare those two essays,
and profit by a consideration of the discrepancy.

The curious inadvertence by which Eliot makes
'urbanity' cover too much parallels that by which he does
the like with 'the virtues of good prose'. And this brings
me back to the observation that he clearly fails to realize
how inseparably in eighteenth-century verse, and with
what significance, those virtues, where they are to be
found, are associated with politeness. It was to bring out
the force of 'politeness' here, and the momentousness of
the association, that I referred back to Marvell's urbanity,
and to the fact that, in so short a time, it was replaced by
something so different.

In its reduction of the possibilities of literary expression
to the prose mode the eighteenth century restricted poets
to cultivating the 'prose virtues'. But 'prose virtues' in
that age entailed, where verse was in question, a peculiarly
insistent politeness. Eliot, in the passage I will read in a
moment, misdirects when instead of 'polite' he says
'courtly'. The 'positive culture' he speaks of had no

reference to any court: the cultural centres it related to in its guise of politeness—for the 'positiveness' *was*, as social civilization, the politeness—were rather the *salon*, the coffee-house and the club. This is what Eliot says:

> The eighteenth century in English verse is not, after Pope, Swift, Prior, and Gay, an age of courtly verse. It seems more like an age of retired country clergymen and schoolmasters. ... And it is intolerably poetic. Instead of working out the proper form for its matter, when it has any, and informing verse with prose virtues, it merely applies the magniloquence of Milton or the neatness of Pope to matter which is wholly unprepared for it; so that what the writers have to say always appears surprised at the way in which they choose to say it.

I might start by commenting that the matter of *Ash-Wednesday* would have appeared surprised had Eliot chosen to apply prose virtues to *it*. But no—what *is* the 'matter' of *Ash-Wednesday*? As I shall point out in my own way later, the poems of *Ash-Wednesday* don't admit of paraphrase. What, validly, Eliot is saying is that in good eighteenth-century verse prose virtues have been applied to matter for which—*this* is what 'informing verse with prose virtues' means—they constitute the proper form. And Johnson's matter is indeed suited to the prose virtues he applies to it, and his poem stands out impressively in the poetic poverty of the century after Pope. But that recognition takes nothing from the truth that the 'positive culture' had no place for the distinctively poetic use of language, the exploratory-creative, exemplified supremely by Shakespeare, and that Johnson's kind of success had the remotest of bearings on Eliot's own task—that of vindicating the poet's function, and showing that a poet might even in our time be as creatively important as a distinguished novelist. Johnson is certainly not courtly, but he would have been surprised, I think, to be told that his mode wasn't properly to be called 'polite'. The word in any case implies an overtly social context—or setting—of communication, and a deference towards the conventions of a congenial social culture. And the poetry of the prose virtues in general insists that what (as Eliot puts it) the poet 'has to say' must be suited to a mode that implies overtly social and 'civilized' presentation: experience that doesn't lend itself to such treatment is implicitly told that it doesn't exist, or is of no consequence.

Instead of trying to explain further what I mean by saying that the 'positive culture', in essential intention, eliminated creativity, I will end with a reference to Blake. That will serve the need for economy that goes with my special purpose, which (let me say again) is to suggest as effectively as I can how I conceive the scope, spirit and lines of literary study in face of the problem I have discussed. Blake, in making his protest against the world of Locke and Newton, found it natural to see an enemy of what he stood for in Johnson too. For his protest was a protest of the individual sensibility, and an insistence on the individual experience. His rebellion against what for him was the ethos of Newton and Locke was a vindication of that which can't be treated mathematically or quantitatively, since it is 'there' only in individual lives—particulars, that is, that can't be added to one another, or averaged, or generalized, or abstracted, and in whom alone creativeness resides. His great creative achievement was to redeem the English language for the expression of an intensely individual sensibility; by which I mean that he reversed what happened when the Augustan age set in and the emphasis came to be laid heavily on the social: a man is a social being. Yes, he inescapably is; but, as the movement and life of Blake's finest lyrics insist implicitly with such power, a man is an individual, and his individuality is his reality. And with his eye on Locke and Newton, Blake points to the continuity running from the creativeness of perception to the creativeness of the artist, and insists that life, while it *is* life, is of its very nature creative.

Eliot's essay on Blake is a distinguished one, and at one time it seemed to me that he made the important points. But he doesn't make the one that I now want most to make—meaning it as an incitement to thought, exploratory reading, and personal judgment on the part of the student and his maturer collaborators. The Romantic movement was a very complex thing, and complex in its legacy; and, as the student will increasingly realize (if he is not wasting his time), to try and define the movement and the legacy in terms of some 'romanticism' is not profitable. The idea that Blake has some definitive and directing, 'wisdom' to impart seems to me unprofitable too, and absurd; but I have more and more settled down to the conviction that he stands for a new sense of human responsibility, and that this is the Romantic era's great permanent contribution. Unlike Shelley, he is not a naïve idealist; there is no luxury of self-pity in his concern for humanity. In a way not generally thought of as belonging to the Romantic inspiration, he is a realist. With his penetrating insight into the human psyche, his integrity and his courage, he finds himself contemplating—and wrestling with— problems of disharmony and conflict for which he can see no solution.

Yet if he is not an optimist, neither is he a pessimist, and the religious spirit so strong in him doesn't tend towards fatalism or resignation. It expresses itself in the confidence, unquestioning but un-hubristic, that the creative life in man will be justified in its positive refusal to be resigned. The contrast of Blake to Bentham may serve to enforce the main point I have been trying to make. You could hardly attribute a religious spirit to the Benthamite inspiration. And the sense of human responsibility that Blake represents is what we desperately need, to supplement, correct and guide—in sum, subdue to the service of life—a victorious, cock-a-hoop and hardly questioned Benthamism.

Permanent contribution? How, in the field of literary studies, would one start to justify that suggestion? Well, Dickens is called a Romantic novelist, and with more than one kind of reason; and it is plain to me that we are contemplating the most important way in which Dickens is 'Romantic' when we consider the greatness of *Little Dorrit*. I mustn't now go off into a discussion of Dickens and his relation to Blake. But I will permit myself to say that if one man may be said to have created the modern novel, it was Dickens, and it is absurd (though it happens a great deal) for a university student of English literature to be without some intelligent acquaintance with him. And the student should know that the line runs from Dickens to D. H. Lawrence, Eliot's (*not* George Eliot's) great opposite.

I intend to discuss Eliot's own poetic achievement next. And I thought it well to put myself, as I have done, in a position to say that the attitude towards life and humanity defined in the work that showed how a modern poet might rival a major novelist as a serious artist is very different from that in relation to which I have associated Blake, Dickens and Lawrence. You hardly needed reminding of that. But I shall no doubt convey a strong admiration for Eliot's work as a poet, and I would rather that, from the start, you didn't suppose me to have adopted for myself the attitude, the ethos, the spirit of it. I am secure against that now, I hope: my comments on Blake and Dickens were—as for my purpose they had to be—so decidedly and essentially *not* neutral.

IV
Why 'Four Quartets' matters in a Technologico-Benthamite Age

WHY '*FOUR QUARTETS*' MATTERS IN A TECHNOLOGICO-BENTHAMITE AGE

To attempt an appreciation of what Eliot achieved in poetry is to enforce and develop the case I put about the 18th century, the prose 'virtues', and the excessive generality of his dictum. As I said, accounting for the excess, he had his eye on the dream-world vagueness of Morris and on the associated characteristics of English poetry from Tennyson to Swinburne. But his own corrective effort as a poet against the tradition of 'soul' was very far from being towards the prose 'virtues' in any sense, or the eighteenth century—which had completed and perpetuated the dissociation. Perpetuated: for when we ask how it was that out of the achievements, so different each from the others, of the great Romantic geniuses, which do represent the finer consciousness of the age, there should have emerged the institutional sensibility (the 'poetical') that Arnold's formulation records, an important part of the answer is given in the confidence with which, by way of defining true poetry, he classes Dryden and Pope as 'classics of our prose' (their verse was conceived and composed, not in the 'soul', but in their 'wits'): a complementary phenomenon of dissociation replaces the earlier. Poetry *was* literature —'the crown of literature', Arnold said in 1887, writing on *Anna Karenina*; the novel was not, and the major creative drive went there, where the relation between experience and art was open and unprejudiced, and it was possible for Dickens to be Shakespearian. And

Dickens was the kind of genius who makes all the difference.

It will have been gathered from the emphasis I have laid on *Four Quartets* that I think it time that a different account of Eliot's poetic achievement was given from that which is current—from any that seems to be current. At any rate, it would be a satisfaction to me to think I might some day be able to look back and feel that I had had a little to do with his ceasing to be thought of primarily as the poet of *The Waste Land*. Since his death I have read and re-read the collected poems in order that I might give the fairest, the most justly definitive, account of his achievement that could be got into an hour's discourse[1]—which, I must add in haste, has not been my purpose for to-day. Writing that critique I by-passed *The Waste Land*, finding, in the pressing need for economy, that I could say what most asked to be said without devoting to it much more than a passing allusion.

Of course, we were right in the 1920s to be immensely impressed by that now famous and familiar poem, but I think we attributed a status as an organic work to it that it doesn't justify, and a representative significance it hasn't. I won't develop those judgments now, but save my time for the strictly necessary, and, in quoting the conclusion of the critique I have mentioned, say that, as I had intimated, it was the succession of poems from 'The Hollow Men' that I had in mind. 'The constituent things'—this was my closing sentence—'are in their concentration so completely what they are, the development is so unforeseeable, and yet so compelling in its logic, that the whole body of the poetry affects us as one astonishing major work'.

[1] See *Lectures in America* by F. R. and Q. D. Leavis (Chatto & Windus).

'The Hollow Men' marks a new development in Eliot.
It clearly asks to be seen as the prelude to *Ash-Wednesday*,
which in the collected poems it immediately precedes;
but not merely because of that, and not (this is important)
because it strikes any religious note. The newness is
obvious enough and the nature of the newness: there is
no irony in 'The Hollow Men', and no revulsion, unless
against the self, implicitly judged to be in some sense a
failure[1], the judgment being unmistakably there in the
reference to 'those' who, unlike 'us', have 'crossed with
direct eyes':

> *Those who have crossed*
> *With direct eyes, to death's other Kingdom*
> *Remember us—if at all—not as lost*
> *Violent souls, but only*
> *As the hollow men*
> *The stuffed men.*

The note carries on into what immediately follows in
the next section, where that which 'death's other Kingdom' is contrasted with appears as 'death's dream
Kingdom'. It is the evocation of the peculiar nostalgic
pang, the impotent yearning, into which this leads that
I want to call attention to.

> *Eyes I dare not meet in dreams*
> *In death's dream kingdom*
> *These do not appear:*
> *There, the eyes are*
> *Sunlight on a broken column*
> *There, is a tree swinging*
> *And voices are*
> *In the wind's singing*
> *More distant and more solemn*
> *Than a fading star*

[1] Cf: D. W. Harding's comments in *Experience into Words*, page 127.

I find it something more than a mere personal idio-syncrasy that this for me associates very closely with a passage in the penultimate paragraph of *The Waste Land*.

> *We think of the key, each in his prison*
> *Thinking of the key, each confirms a prison*
> *Only at nightfall, aethereal rumours*
> *Revive for a moment a broken Coriolanus*

That, though very different, is not essentially at odds with the earlier reference to Coriolanus in 'A Cooking Egg':

> *I shall not want Honour in Heaven*
> *For I shall meet Sir Philip Sidney*
> *And have talk with Coriolanus*
> *And other heroes of that kidney*

The irony here conveys criticism of some kind (I imagine) of the Honour, the Pride, that the name of Coriolanus evokes, but the later passages—for those from *The Waste Land* and 'The Hollow Men' do really, I think, associate and register one and the same development—suggest a new sense in the poet that there was too much Coriolanus in the irony. There is no touch of superiority in 'The Hollow Men'; the poet himself is too much the broken Coriolanus to be ironical in any way, or to enjoy self-dramatization, cynical or otherwise. Nor does he revert to the old kind of irony in the unfinished sequence he called, significantly, *Coriolan*, though the account I have given of those poems is that they are the nearest thing we can expect in our age to distinguished satiric poetry.

The figure of Coriolanus was lodged deep in Eliot's imagination (there's an oddly revealing reference to the play—along with an equally odd one to *Antony and Cleopatra*—in the essay on *Hamlet* that I shall discuss later). But at the moment it is that highly specific emotional quality I am concerned with which in the passage of 'The Hollow Men' made me think of the Coriolanus note in the close of *The Waste Land*. The point I want to make regards the nature of Eliot's genius. He has this power which Arnold would have had no difficulty in recognizing as that of a poet—a great poet: the power of giving concrete definition to (that is, of seizing and evoking in words and rhythms) feelings and apprehensions—the focal core with the elusive aura—that have seemed to him peculiarly significant elements in his most private experience. But what goes with this power in the fully mature Eliot is the power of searching and sustained thought; thought that is not a matter of reflecting poetically (to use Eliot's own dismissing phrase), but thought that requires for its definition and conduct means and procedures that are essentially poetic.

Four Quartets is a feat of disciplined thinking, but one a culture that imposed the prose 'virtues' couldn't have produced—or recognized. It required a capacity for intensely private or non-social (or non-currency) experience—which amounts to saying, for bringing to expression in language what language doesn't readily lend itself to; to say which, of course, is to recognize that the distinction, 'public—private', ceases to be a clear antithesis and begins to present difficulties once it is taken outside the limits of commonsense use. We are brought here to the importance for humanity of the major poet, the original creative writer, who is always concerned with creating what is in some sense a public world, or, to put it in another way, with modifying the 'public world' (I use inverted commas this time) as he finds it.

Since our concern was speech, and speech impelled us
To purify the dialect of the tribe

'To purify the dialect of the tribe'—thus, you remember, the ghostly fellow-poet 'Both intimate and
unidentifiable' to Eliot in the air-raid section of 'Little
Gidding'. It is a mark of Eliot's peculiar importance to
us—that is, of his major status as a poet of our time—
that he should have had his distinctive preoccupation
with language. I am thinking of the preoccupation that,
with the pressure behind it, is expressed here, in the
opening of section V of 'East Coker':

So here I am, in the middle way, having had twenty
  years—
Twenty years largely wasted, the years of l'entre
  deux guerres—
Trying to learn to use words, and every attempt
Is a wholly new start, and a different kind of failure
Because one has only learnt to get the better of words
For the thing one no longer has to say, or the way in
  which
One is no longer disposed to say it

The poet of 'The Hollow Men' was clearly a man
driven by a desperate need; a need to apprehend with
sureness a reality that should compel belief, claim allegi-
ance and create a centre of significance. The association,
or identification, of the quest driven by such a need
with the unendingly resourceful struggle to 'get the
better of words' determines the way and the sense in
which Eliot's later poetry is religious.

Now the mode of *Ash-Wednesday* differs very obviously
from that of *Four Quartets*. Nowhere in it is there anything that challenges the full attention of the waking mind

in the blunt prose-like way of the opening of 'Burnt Norton', where we seem to be starting on a metaphysical essay. You might be inclined to say that the insistently liturgical element and the accompanying character of the rhythm—isn't it incantatory?—make a thinking attention to the sense impossible; at any rate, that they don't demand it; rather, they discourage it. If you said that, you would be showing that, though you might sincerely say you had enjoyed the poetry, you hadn't really read it. There would be no reason why you should quarrel with Anglo-Catholic expositors who make the poetry something utterly different from what it is, which is something utterly different as religious poetry from (say) Herbert's. For it is in answering the question, 'In what sense is *this* religious poetry?', that one has to take account of its insistent challenge to the thinking—the pondering, distinguishing, relating—mind.

It is, with the scrupulousness of genius, non-affirmative in the spirit defined by Eliot himself in these lines from 'East Coker':

> *I said to my soul, be still, and wait without hope*
> *For hope would be hope for the wrong thing; wait*
> *without love*
> *For love would be love of the wrong thing; there is*
> *yet faith*
> *But the faith and the love and the hope are all in the*
> *waiting.*
> *Wait without thought, for you are not ready for*
> *thought . . .*

These lines give you the mode, or the region, to which *Ash-Wednesday* belongs. You might perhaps retort that the last line contradicts what I have been saying about the poem. But you must not take the line—an injunction

and a statement—by itself; you must take the half-dozen
lines together; and it is plain from them, even apart
from their context, that what Eliot is saying is something that couldn't have been said in a way that would
satisfy a logician; and that the ostensible self-contradiction
of the passage in 'But the faith and the love and the hope
are all in the waiting' isn't a self-contradiction. The
simplest way of justifying that statement of mine is to
examine a constituent poem of *Ash-Wednesday*. The distinctive mode of the whole work is exploratory, tentative
and testing, and is so in the spirit of those lines from
'East Coker' I have just read. The poet's desperate need
compels him to avoid even the show of affirmation: he
hopes that the affirmation will make itself—he hopes with
that kind of hope which, in the 'East Coker' passage, he
says is not hope. But although the poetry is non-affirmative, it expresses a nisus towards what is represented by
the liturgical element, and, more generally, the positively
religious and Christian note. 'This—this need, this
aspiration, this effort—is *in* me, it affirms itself': that is
what the poetry implicitly says. The poet no longer
strives to strive towards such things, but there *is* a kind
of striving, a profound unwilled set of the whole being—
a nisus, I called it. The nature of this, and what I mean
by 'unwilled' (I too have to use words, and I am not a
poet) is given in the opening lines of the poem.

> *Because I do not hope to turn again*
> *Because I do not hope*
> *Because I do not hope to turn*
> *Desiring this man's gift and that man's scope*
> *I no longer strive to strive towards such things*

—if striving involves the will, and willing involves self-
assertion and the desire to exalt the self, then there is to

be no more striving. The irony of the parenthesis that immediately follows is directed against the self; even in self-abnegation there may be the taint of self-exaltation or self-approval, as everyone knows. I have my eye on the 'agèd eagle'.

The kind of full waking attention the poem calls for is apparent in the part that shifts of tone play in the definition of attitude—that is, in the meaning; a part exemplified by that parenthesis and the shifts it entails from what went before and to what follows:

> I no longer strive to strive towards such things
> (Why should the agèd eagle stretch its wings?)
> Why should I mourn
> The vanished power of the usual reign?

Breaking a general resolution I had come to, I will permit myself to comment that we know as a matter of historical fact that the power of the 'usual reign' had not vanished for good, and that Eliot was, among other things, to go on to spend a great deal of his life writing those embarrassing plays; embarrassing because, aiming at success in the theatre, with the applause of the best people and a kudos that a man of his kind of distinction should surely not be very much concerned for, they nevertheless make an intensely earnest show of engaging the deeper preoccupations of the great poet. But it is never Eliot's genius that functions when he is conscious of the social world, the world where social pressures, social suggestion and social 'civilization' work (especially on the insecure) in the most insidious ways, and it is to the social world that an admirer of his genius must judge his interest in the theatre to have belonged. There *was*—this is an essential datum—an insecurity; the fact has to be recognized in an appreciation of his genius, which manifests itself in the heroic integrity of his poetic career. To say 'heroic' is to recognize the peculiar inner resistances and disloyalties and subversions the genius had to contend with, and the peculiar isolation in which it worked. And for myself I feel that the time has come now to dwell mainly on the admiration and gratitude due for the creative upshot of the battle. But there clearly was, behind the achievement, a battle, and an endless one. Eliot's poetic technique is a technique for sincerity: I shall at any rate, perhaps, have given an edge to that proposition.

To come back now to 'Perch' io non spero'—which is the title the opening poem of *Ash-Wednesday* had when I first read it, in a very *chic* French publication, *Commerce*, with a French translation *en regard*. One has to be on one's guard against being confidently definitive, but it is clear, I think, that

> *The vanished power of the usual reign*

stands in antithesis to the 'infirm glory' and the 'transitory power' of the next paragraph:

> *Because I do not hope to know again*
> *The infirm glory of the positive hour*
> *Because I do not think*
> *Because I know I shall not know*
> *The one veritable transitory power*
> *Because I cannot drink*
> *There, where trees flower and springs flow,*
>   *for there is nothing again . . .*

The poem is clearly invoking here the remembered experiences and intimations, the 'intersections' (in his

own phrase) of the timeless with time, that play so great
a part in the processes by which Eliot in *Four Quartets*,

Thus devoted, concentrated in purpose

—'purpose' here being something that has been set over
against will—endeavours 'to construct something upon
which to rejoice'. You'll notice the inconsequence (it's a
good instance of Eliot's use of logic in his 'constructing',
for the blankly *conscious* inconsequence *is* a use) with
which that phrase, introduced with 'consequently', is
made to clinch the passage (the one that comes next):

> *Because I know that time is always time*
> *And place is always and only place*
> *And what is actual is actual only for one time*
> *And only for one place*
> *I rejoice that things are as they are and*
> *I renounce the blessed face*
> *And renounce the voice*
> *Because I cannot hope to turn again*
> *Consequently I rejoice, having to construct something*
> *Upon which to rejoice*

'Clinch', I said, but it isn't after all the right word,
because the paragraph, with only one comma for punctuation, goes on in its non-logical way for eight more lines.
The propositional form of what are offered us as propositions is essential to the poetry, to the 'constructive'
organization, but, as the absence of punctuation implicitly
avows, the 'consequence' with which they follow one
another, the relation in which they stand, is not logical.

I mustn't, however, spend longer on this kind of
detailed discussion of *Ash-Wednesday*. My purpose in
these lectures doesn't permit it, not aiming at, or permit-
ting, an expository critique of Eliot's poetry. It is to lay
some emphases and make some points in order to enforce

my contention about the opportunities presented by
Eliot's work in relation to the problems that literary
study, if we think it important, faces us with at the
university. I have made my limited points about the
mode of *Ash-Wednesday*. For all the suggestion of incantatory rhythm, the poetry demands the fullest and
most delicate attention of the waking mind. And the
meanings are of a kind that doesn't admit of paraphrase
—in a doctrinal commentary, or in any other way. You
have already the clear signs of that intense interest in
language—in what words and syntactical conventions do
to dictate thought and disguise or transmute basic intention, perception and apprehension—which has its most
developed outcome in *Four Quartets*.

Perhaps I had better now indicate a little more directly
how I would justify my associating the special importance
I attribute to Eliot's poetry with the fact that the civilization we live in is what it is. As I hope I have done
something to bring out, the peculiar intensity of Eliot's
absorption in 'trying to use words' is the intensity of his
need. The nature of that need as a distinctive portent of
our time—that is, as something more than merely
personal—gets direct expression in the two poems of
the unfinished *Coriolan* sequence. I remarked earlier that
they seem to me to be as near to major satiric poetry as
anything we are likely to get in our age. I don't say they
are satiric, because the word 'satire', I think, entails the
idea of critical animus, and criticism implies standards—
positive standards. The great age of satire was the Queen
Anne Augustan, which enjoyed a magnificent confidence,
based on the consensus regarding ends, values and the
business of life that produced its great poem in the
fourth book of the *Dunciad*. Our age is the antithesis of

that. If it tends to anything like a consensus, the consensus is not of a kind that helps towards distinguished
satiric creation. And here, one might say, we have the
theme of 'Difficulties of a Statesman':

> *Cry what shall I cry*
> *All flesh is grass: comprehending*
> *The Companions of the Bath, the Knights of the*
>   *British Empire, the Cavaliers,*
> *O Cavaliers! of the Legion of Honour,*
> *The Order of the Black Eagle (1st and 2nd class),*
> *And the Order of the Rising Sun.*
> *Cry cry what shall I cry*
> *The first thing to do is to form the committees:*
> *The consultative councils, the standing committees,*
>   *select committees and sub-committees.*
> *One secretary will do for several committees.*
> *What shall I cry*

It will be seen that what Eliot recoils from here is not
what is represented by Sweeney, object of a protest
associated with the characteristic sexual disgust, or by
'The red-eyed scavengers' who are creeping 'From
Kentish Town and Golder's Green', but by meaninglessness; the loss of significance, of satisfying ends and
of any adequate concern for them, or of the power of
adequate concern, in the elaboration of the machinery—
meaninglessness and unreality. Instead of the positive
references of the satirist you have the way in which
meaninglessness and unreality are evoked as the nightmare insanity of the actual. That is, the positive—if the
word may be used here—is present as deprivation and
the felt irresistible need.

There are closely related passages, as you know, in
Four Quartets. I will read one of them, for it's the approach

to *Four Quartets* I am preoccupied with, and I have my eye on the problem that for me is one of delicacy. The passage I want to read is the first part of Section III of 'East Coker':

> *O dark dark dark. They all go into the dark,*
> *The vacant interstellar spaces, the vacant into the*
> *vacant,*
> *The captains, merchant bankers, eminent men of*
> *letters,*
> *The generous patrons of art, the statesmen and the*
> *rulers,*
> *Distinguished civil servants, chairmen of many*
> *committees,*
> *Industrial lords and petty contractors, all go into the*
> *dark,*
> *And dark the Sun and Moon, and the Almanach de*
> *Gotha*
> *And the Stock Exchange Gazette, the Directory of*
> *Directors,*
> *And cold the sense and lost the motive of action.*
> *And we all go with them, into the silent funeral,*
> *Nobody's funeral, for there is no one to bury.*
> *I said to my soul, be still, and let the dark come upon*
> *you*
> *Which shall be the darkness of God*

You see why I passed to this from 'Difficulties of a Statesman'. And you can see the difference,—or differences. Even if you weren't acquainted with the context you could tell that the poet's presence in the poem is much completer and that his undertaking is much more comprehensive and pertinacious. In fact, compared with what he is doing here, in *Four Quartets*, 'Difficulties of a Statesman' is an ejaculation. One can see why Eliot, for a poet of his genius, was so unabundant a producer. The labour, the patience, the sustained and renewed integrity, that went to the composing of *Four Quartets* are unimaginable. But immediately, about the passage I've just read, there's a further comparative point I have to make: this poetry is insistently religious in pre-occupation in a way that raises for a commentator like myself a problem of delicacy.

It's not mere modesty in me; not the fact that I'm so decidedly not unaware of certain deficiencies of equipment. It's that I'm bent on getting full recognition for the peculiar importance Eliot has for us in a technologico-Benthamite civilization. I've insisted how different his religious poetry is from what his theologizing expositors tend to make it. I've insisted on its extreme continence of affirmation, and on the way in which it depends on the creative presentation of what compels a response that is recognition, recognition that is not distinguishable from assent. I'll quote briefly here from what I wrote long ago[1] with what was then the latest part of *Four Quartets* in front of me:

'The poetry from *Ash-Wednesday* onwards doesn't say, "I believe", or, "I know", or "Here is the truth": it is positive in direction, but not positive in that way (the difference from Dante is extreme). It is a searching of experience, a spiritual discipline, a technique for sincerity—for giving "sincerity" a meaning. The pre-occupation is with establishing from among the illusions, evanescences and unrealities of life in time (modern life) an apprehension of an assured reality—a reality that, though necessarily apprehended *in* time, is not of it.'

Yes, that seems to me an account of *Four Quartets*

[1] Reprinted as Appendix I in *Education and the University.*

that can be enforced in detailed analysis, and it seems to me that the poetry so described must—false preconceptions as to the working having been got out of the way—have a profound effect on anyone capable of reading poetry.

But wholly non-affirmative? Some may see reason to question the propriety of that description. If this were a series of lectures on *Four Quartets* I should spend a good deal of the time examining the ways in which the poetry does its positive work. All I can do on the present occasion and in these conditions is to remind you of the nature of Eliot's art by quoting a passage, and I do it in order that my answer to the question I proposed ('wholly non-affirmative?') may have some, at least, of its due force. The passage I shall read is the first part of Section V of 'Burnt Norton', but I will start with the last sentence of the brief preceding paragraph, which gives us the yearningly tentative apprehension and evocation of the real:

> *After the kingfisher's wing*
> *Has answered light to light, and is silent, the light is*
> *   still*
> *At the still point of the turning world.*

V

> *Words move, music moves*
> *Only in time; but that which is only living*
> *Can only die. Words, after speech, reach*
> *Into the silence. Only by the form, the pattern,*
> *Can words or music reach*
> *The stillness, as a Chinese jar still*
> *Moves perpetually in its stillness.*
> *Not the stillness of the violin, while the note lasts,*
> *Not that only, but the co-existence,*

Or say that the end precedes the beginning,
And the end and the beginning were always there
Before the beginning and after the end.
And all is always now. Words strain,
Crack and sometimes break, under the burden,
Under the tension, slip, slide, perish,
Decay with imprecision, will not stay in place,
Will not stay still.

This is one of those modes of *Four Quartets* which most plainly and insistently demand the reader's full intellectual attention. The series of propositions and the way in which they are related are such that we can certainly say that the passage has the prose virtues. How it is we should know it for poetry even apart from its context may seem at first not easily said. But of course we are not, in fact, unacquainted with the context, and we feel strongly the current that flows through the passage, giving it something so different from the detachment suggested by the words 'abstract' and 'theory'; giving it the effect of a wrestling with experience that engages the whole being and on which issues of the greatest emotional and spiritual moment are felt to depend. The passage I read runs into this, the close of 'Burnt Norton':

The detail of the pattern is movement,
As in the figure of the ten stairs.
Desire itself is movement
Not in itself desirable;
Love is itself unmoving,
Only the cause and end of movement,
Timeless, and undesiring
Except in the aspect of time
Caught in the form of limitation

127

Between un-being and being.
Sudden in a shaft of sunlight
Even while the dust moves
There rises the hidden laughter
Of children in the foliage
Quick now, here, now, always—
Ridiculous the waste sad time
Stretching before and after.

The play—a creative play—with the word 'still' is the very opposite of a game: it registers a habit of intense philosophic meditation, emotionally impelled, for a purpose that could only be achieved creatively. The purpose of 'Burnt Norton' is achieved by a marvellous interplay of diverse means in the poem as a whole, some of which very much more invite the description of emotional and evocative than the passage I read. I have somewhere[1] given my own brief characterization of the poem, but I will quote rather what D. W. Harding says about it in *Experience Into Words:*

'One could say, perhaps, that the poem takes the place of the ideas of "regret" and "eternity". Where in ordinary speech we should have to use those words, and hope by conversational trial and error to obviate the grosser misunderstandings, this poem is a newly created concept, equally abstract, but vastly more exact and rich in meaning. It makes no statement. It is no more "about" anything than "love" is about anything: it is a linguistic creation. And the creation of a new concept, with all the assimilation and communication of experience that that involves, is perhaps his greatest of linguistic achievements.'

Harding's account, one to be pondered ('yes, but—')

[1] See *Education and the University*, Appendix I.

against the poem, makes plain what he means when he calls 'Burnt Norton' abstract. I say this because the emphasis that I, for my purpose, would have in view in describing the poem would rest on the characteristic that I think of as concreteness. What I mean is that one can't read it and take it in as a poem in a detached intellectual way. In taking the 'communication' of the 'idea' (I use Harding's words) one goes through a different process from the mastering of a logical disquisition; the whole being is involved, and one is compelled, in the taking, to achieve a new realization of the nature of experience. And that realization isn't, and couldn't be, a mere matter of interest in theory. It involves one's basic attitudes and one's habits of thought and valuation. That is what I mean by saying that no one could take the communication of 'Burnt Norton' and not know, with decisive force, that the spiritual Philistinism of the world we live in is menacingly anti-human, or inertly accept 'a rising standard of living' as an adequate account of human ends and needs.

Since I am not philosophically or theologically qualified, but still think, modestly (I hope) that we, in the literary-critical field, have our rights and opportunities, or, rather, responsibilities (subject, of course, to possible correction from specialist disciplines), I will refer here to a passage in a chapter (to which I shall come back later) of D. H. Lawrence—'The Theatre' in *Twilight in Italy*.

'We are tempted' [this was fifty years ago, well before the rise of Hitler], 'like Nietzsche, to return back to the old pagan Infinite, to say that is supreme. Or we are inclined, like the English and the Pragmatist, to say. "There is no Infinite, there is no Absolute". The only Absolute is expediency, the only reality is sensation, and momentariness. But we may say this, even act on it. . . . But we never believe it.'

The key-word there, as (I suggest) in the discussion of *Four Quartets*, is 'reality'. And it is illuminating to see with what kind of context Lawrence gives that word, together with 'Absolute' and 'Infinite', the force required for the expression of his insight and his thought. The context is a discussion of Shakespeare's *Hamlet* (to which I shall revert); and Lawrence, in his criticism of a major creative work, is, in his strength as a critic and a thinker, essentially the creative writer whose genius we know— the creative writer being consummately a critic. His thought can be taken by those who know that creative works are modes of thought.

What, in (no doubt) too compressed a way, I am trying to insist on with this reference is the limitation I've set myself to observe in my own delicate kind of commentary; or, rather, the nature of the centre from which I offer it. My centre is in the field of literary studies—literary criticism. Concerned for the relevance in comment that is the distinctive responsibility of the literary critic, my line has been to talk in terms of the kinds of recognition one finds compelled on one when one cultivates Eliot's religious poetry. And my pre-occupation has been with vindicating the importance I have attributed to Eliot for the purpose I proposed as the theme of these lectures.

I have emphasized Eliot's continence of affirmation. But as we go on through the subsequent quartets we find the specifically Christian note becoming stronger. And towards the end of the third, 'The Dry Salvages', we come finally to this:

> *For most of us, there is only the unattended*
> *Moment, the moment in and out of time,*
> *The distraction fit, lost in a shaft of sunlight*

The wild thyme unseen, or the winter lightning
Or the waterfall, or music heard so deeply
That it is not heard at all, but you are the music
While the music lasts. These are only hints and
  guesses,
Hints followed by guesses; and the rest
Is prayer, observance, discipline, thought and action.
The hint half guessed, the gift half understood, is
  Incarnation.

Is that last sentence non-affirmative? Isn't it explicit affirmation? In form, certainly, and no doubt in the poet's intention too. But the context, it seems to me, gives it something of an interrogative force—or (shall I say) imparts to it something of that element of appeal which characterizes a judgment: 'This is so, isn't it?' And the point I want to make is that I don't think the word comes so charged by what has preceded that it has the clinching inevitability the poet hopes for.

Of course, different readers will report differently. I report what I find. And my concern, which entails an insistence on his utter unlikeness to both Herbert and Dante, is to enforce a given judgment, a given constatation, of the peculiar importance of Eliot's poetry in such an age as ours. It is a concern to make what seems to me the indisputable claim.

The evoking in *Four Quartets* of what we ordinarily call reality as unreal, the astonishing resource with which the ways in which it is unreal are brought home to us, is part of the total process by which our need to recognize values and apprehensions not allowed for by the technologico-Benthamite ethos is enforced. And the enforcing takes a form that compels a close attention to the subtleties of linguistic expression—to the ways in which the conceptual currency may affect the problem of how and what one believes and what believing is, and in which linguistic conventions and habits partly determine experience. That the creative battle to vindicate spiritual values should be associated, as it is in *Four Quartets*, with the subtlest kind of analytic interest in language seems to me a piece of good fortune that we, who are concerned for humane education at a time when linguistic science, or scientific linguistics, is making its victorious advances, have a duty to exploit. For they have, those advances, menacing possibilities for the matters of our concern. Inquire, for instance, what the British Council is doing in the field of *its* jurisdiction.

V
The Necessary Opposite, Lawrence: Illustration—the Opposed Critics on 'Hamlet'

THE NECESSARY OPPOSITE, LAWRENCE: ILLUSTRATION—THE OPPOSED CRITICS ON *HAMLET*

E<small>LIOT</small>'s name has figured a great deal in these lectures, and one of the four has been devoted to his achievement in poetry—about which there is something more I must say. I hope that no one deduces from these facts that I propose to make him the main subject of study in a university English School, or a subject that should bulk in the student's economy on a scale proportionate to the share of attention I have given him. But a misunderstanding of that kind isn't, I think, very probable. I have tried, at any rate, to make plain how I see my undertaking, how I intend it, and how far it is from anything in the nature of laying down a syllabus. Nor have I been offering what I intend to be taken as authoritative literary criticism or literary history. What I am concerned with is something more like a definition of principle, the principle being of such a kind that the defining can't be done in mere general statement. It regards the kind of way in which a problem is to be solved, and the method and spirit (some word between the two is wanted) that 'principle' here portends can be effectively presented only with the aid of exemplification.

When I say 'problem' I am thinking in the first place of the undergraduate faced with that immense field of reading. From the beginning he needs, to fortify him for his inevitably piece-meal approaches—and he should be put on the path to acquiring it as early as possible, some insight into the way in which English literature exists at any time as a living reality, in so far as it does; some grasp of the sense in which the suggestion of the two combined words is justified, in so far as it is—the suggestion that they portend something more than a collection of authors and works and a sequence in time. He needs a principle of life to guide, animate and organize his growing knowledge of English literature; and 'principle' here obviously doesn't mean anything that can be contained in a simple statement: I think of 'principle of life' as something that can't be stated at all.

But one can, with point, say to the student (and the saying is not mere telling):

> There's this good fortune we have in having Eliot, a major poet—*the* great poet of our time—whose criticism, which has been a decisive influence on taste and critical thought, insists, not the less essentially because implicitly, on the relation between his own creative work and the past; throwing out, as it does so, seminal suggestions about the shape of our poetic history. Make the most of him. In becoming intelligent about his creative achievement and the criticism belonging with it you apprehend, you acquire, the active informing principle without which there is little to be got from the protracted study of literature.

The great poet of our time—Eliot is surely that. And he hasn't the kind of immediate contemporaneity that makes a writer unsuitable for formal recognition as a subject of academic study. Yet the academic attention has gone to Yeats, who, it seems to me, is decidedly the lesser poet, and certainly less repaying. Yeats has been for years now both a cult and an industry, and I see it as a strong recommendation of Eliot when I say that nothing like either of these has found its excuse in him, or very well could. The cult and the industry entail taking

Yeats's life-long addiction to the occult and the esoteric, together with the schematisms and the diagrammatics and the symbolical elaborations that were its product, with the kind of seriousness that prescribes earnest study of these last—prescribes it as necessary to the appreciation of Yeats's poetry. But it is not (which isn't the worst that is to be said), and the sanctioned habit leads to much bad criticism, and, for undergraduates, to an expenditure, of time and energy they can't afford—and couldn't even if it were only waste.

There is no equivalent of *A Vision* or *Phases of the Moon* where Eliot is concerned, and in any case a cult is not what I am advocating. Intelligent admiration for him and his work will always be qualified, and I have tried to make plain my conviction to that effect. And I must now say more about the way in which appreciation of the poetic achievement entails limiting judgments, and these entail critical observations about the poet as a man. Up till now I have kept these to a minimum, wishing to emphasize the achievement. But, after all, we are concerned with the profit to be got from the study of it; and a full appreciation of what has been achieved, a full grasp of the significance, entails some realization of what went to it, and of the conditions of the achieving.

It is, under the last head, an essential datum in Eliot's case that he was very early taken up by Bloomsbury— the Bloomsbury that was found in possession of the literary scene when peace-time civilization began again in 1919. It was the Hogarth Press that published *The Waste Land* when it first appeared in book-(or book-let-) form. How completely Eliot was, socially, *of* Bloomsbury I myself didn't realize for many years; but I was very innocent. Today's literary student needn't be innocent in that way, and it is to be desired that he shouldn't be; not only ought he to be intelligent about that literary world—our literary world—in the early history of which Bloomsbury played an important part; there are immediate significances for the critic faced with Eliot. I remarked, admitting the difficulty of defining with any precision what I meant, but communicating it (I hope) sufficiently, that his genius didn't function in the social world. There was a profound insecurity in him, one aspect of which he avows under cover of irony in 'The Love Song of J. Alfred Prufrock' (1917):

> *I have seen the moment of my greatness flicker,*
> *And I have seen the eternal Footman hold my coat*
>   *and snicker,*
> *And in short, I was afraid.*

It is seen in those letters he used to write to *The Times*, in some curious inclusions in *Selected Essays*, and with an obvious disturbing significance in the British Academy lecture on Milton. That for the critic it must be something more than an embarrassing personal trait in a distinguished man is manifest in his docile adhesion to Bloomsbury. It was the marked character of that coterie-milieu to combine pretensions to the custodianship of the higher cultural values with the pride of social distinction —a matter of exclusiveness. It stood, its members felt, supremely for 'civilization'. Eliot—how far, or how deeply, he was conscious of the fact it's impossible to say—was essentially not, in his genius, in resonance with the Bloomsbury ethos, though as a social person he was. He can't have been without some troubling awareness; but he was not a whole man, and the coterie influence, which pervaded the literary world at large and was strong enough to make some deplorable tendencies

respectable, certainly confirmed in him the inner disorder, and the lack of self-knowledge that went with it.

This is apparent in the history of his attitude towards
Lawrence. The antipathy he gave utterance to with such
assured, authoritative and ignorant righteousness was
spontaneous and deeply personal; it came from the
weak, the uncreative—the *anti*-creative—T. S. Eliot, as
he himself confessed later, when fashion had changed;
virtually confessed, for instance, in pronouncing that if
anyone in our time 'had stood for the spirit' (Eliot's own
phrase) it was Lawrence. The fact that Bloomsbury was
with him had made him, in his brave anti-Lawrence
days, take his weakness for his strength, and given him
(to his profound disadvantage) a confidence he wouldn't
otherwise have had.

I am moving, with this piece of history, towards a
critical judgment regarding that poetic achievement about
which I have spoken in such high terms; a judgment I
must make with force and clarity enough to ensure that
my own attitude, the spirit in which I admire, and the
intention with which I have urged the claims of the
achievement as a subject to study, shall not be mis-
conceived. It is to the effect that the admiring, and the
assent that critical admiration carries with it, are to be
understood as having the form, 'Yes, but—' and that
the 'but' is a very serious matter. That the creative Eliot
could not draw on any wholeness of being, or free flow
of life, has consequences for criticism, and the 'social'
poverty of spirit—the unheroism (it led him to call
Lawrence a snob)—was a manifestation of the disunity,
the disability, the inner disorder that characterized him:
there is much significance in its allying itself so readily
with his instinctive animus against Lawrence.

In calling the animus instinctive I mean that it expressed something quite other in himself than intelligence or critical judgment. It expressed something that may properly be called a disorder. As a way of moving further in discussion of this delicate theme, I will quote a sentence I wrote not long ago in explanation of the judgment that the treatment in *The Waste Land* of the dried-up springs and the failure of life hasn't the breadth of significance claimed and asserted by the title and the apparatus of notes: 'The distinctive attitude towards, the feeling about, the relations between men and women that predominates in the poem is the highly personal one we know so well from the earlier poems; the symbolic Waste Land makes itself felt too much as Thomas Stearns Eliot's.' That sentence gives more explicitness to a passing judgment I threw out here the other day.

And this leads me to recall a very early poem of Eliot's—one that, I have read or heard, it gave him no pleasure to be reminded of as his: 'La Figlia Che Piange' (published along with 'Prufrock' and 'The Portrait of a Lady' in 1917). I am fond of the poem, as well as thinking it important, but I will merely, by way of refreshing your memory of its nature, read the closing paragraph:

> *She turned away, but with the autumn weather*
> *Compelled my imagination many days,*
> *Many days and many hours:*
> *Her hair over her arms and her arms full of flowers.*
> *And I wonder how they should have been together!*
> *I should have lost a gesture and a pose.*
> *Sometimes these cogitations still amaze*
> *The troubled midnight and the noon's repose.*

Love unequivocally presented, love that calls for lyrical expression—the poem is unique in the Eliot volume.

Again I will quote a sentence of mine from the critique
I have referred to,[1] in which my aim was to concentrate
on defining the superb total achievement; 'The general
truth about him is that he can contemplate the relations
between men and women only with revulsion or disgust—
unless with the aid of Dante.' In that last phrase, of
course, I was thinking of *Ash-Wednesday* and of the part
played there by experience such as 'La Figlia Che
Piange' records in the process by which, 'having to
construct something upon which to rejoice', he seeks to
build up, confirm and define his apprehension of a
spiritual reality. Love, human love, a memory coming
under that head and become an established and deep-
lying emotional centre—a spiritual value—exists for him
as the gleam of a reality to be sought with disciplined
devotion. The place in *Ash-Wednesday* where the memory
(a word that acquires a special meaning in *Four Quartets*)
appears directly is in the third poem, which I first read
under the title of 'Som de l'escalina'. I had better read
the passage out in its context, so as to remind you just
how the memory comes in—which is the point:

> There were no more faces and the stair was dark,
> Damp, jaggèd, like an old man's mouth drivelling,
>   beyond repair,
> Or the toothed gullet of an agèd shark.
> At the first turning of the third stair
> Was a slotted window bellied like the fig's fruit
> And beyond the hawthorn blossom and a pasture scene
> The broadbacked figure drest in blue and green
> Enchanted the maytime with an antique flute.
> Blown hair is sweet, brown hair over the mouth
>   blown,
> Lilac and brown hair;

[1] *Lectures in America.*

Distraction, music of the flute, stops and steps of the
  mind over the third stair,
Fading, fading; strength beyond hope and despair
Climbing the third stair.

That needs no comment. In the fourth poem, the one
that follows, you can see the memory of love, not now
overtly that, transmuted with Dante's aid into something
that is spiritual in a way that offers more decisively to
leave the mundane behind. It is the sixth and last poem
that yields, I think, most; I mean, yields *me* most for
my present purpose, which is to define the 'Yes, but—'
I want to leave against Eliot—the great Eliot whom I
admire.

Although I do not hope to turn again
Although I do not hope
Although I do not hope to turn

Wavering between the profit and the loss
In this brief transit where the dreams cross
The dreamcrossed twilight between birth and dying
(Bless me father) though I do not wish to wish these
  things
From the wide window towards the granite shore
The white sails still fly seaward, seaward flying
Unbroken wings

And the lost heart stiffens and rejoices
In the lost lilac and the lost sea voices
And the weak spirit quickens to rebel
For the bent golden-rod and the lost sea smell
Quickens to recover
The cry of quail and the whirling plover
And the blind eye creates
The empty forms between the ivory gates
And smell renews the salt savour of the sandy earth

142

The nature of the musical interplay that organizes the complexity into a poem is introduced in the fourth line:

Wavering between the profit and the loss

And the 'wavering' is focused into concentrations and simultaneities of equivocation that you can put your finger on in the 'lost':

And the lost heart stiffens and rejoices
In the lost lilac and the lost sea voices . . .

—Lost as in 'lost soul'? Lost, certainly, in that it 'stiffens' to 'rebel'. It does that when it 'rejoices' in a positive nostalgia for the 'lost lilac' and the 'lost sea voices': 'lost' here is unmistakably a rebellious word: the 'weak spirit quickens' in rebellion for that which in memory, is life and the renewal of life. 'Rebel', of course, along with 'stiffens', condemns, but there is no simple and flat condemnation in the effect. For—as the four quartets subtly and intensively illustrate—these memories play an indispensable part in the effort to build up the sure apprehension of a spiritual reality, a reality that transcends time.

It's not the play of ambiguity and equivocation in itself that, at the moment, I see as significant (though it *has* its significance, and it gives us a magnificent example of Eliot's poetic genius). My immediate point is that here, where the genius works with such power, and the evocation of a pre-Waste-Land world in which trees flower and springs flow and the wings are unbroken and the heart rejoices, is so poignantly strong, I find myself reflecting: 'And yet the memories are all of the same kind, in the sense that the intensity they have is remoteness and the kind is not one that suggests a rich, or representative, human experience (compare what Blake does with those lyrics of his). The passage, in fact, prompts me to suggest that there is a commentary asking to be made on the great but highly specific part played in Eliot's religious poetry by memories evoked out of childhood. In 'Som de l'escalina' the 'lilac' goes, we note, with 'brown hair'—'brown hair over the mouth blown', but what is more significant than any simple emotional recall is the prepotence in *Ash-Wednesday* of Dante's Beatrice. There is certainly profound significance there—I am thinking of the story of the boy Dante and Bice Portinari and of the interest Eliot has shown in it.[1]

I have been moving towards the overt judgment: Eliot's poetry hasn't a rich human experience behind it. It reveals, rather, a restriction; it comes, indeed, out of a decided poverty. The occasion to explain how I would justify that word and the judgment it clinches is offered by the close of that last poem in *Ash-Wednesday*:

> *Sister, mother*
> *And spirit of the river, spirit of the sea,*
> *Suffer me not to be separated*
> *And let my cry come unto Thee.*

'That, a psychologist would say', (comments D. W. Harding) 'is the cry of the weaned child', and Harding, himself a psychologist, doesn't dissociate himself. Now I don't think that any adverse criticism is necessarily involved in the observation that Eliot's creative music (you know well enough what I mean by that phrase) does use the given element of human experience. The actual comment I am led to make takes me back to a note I had ready, but have put aside, on 'Marina', a poem that I like very much indeed—in fact, I like it best of all the poems. The Marina is the heroine of Shakespeare's

[1] See *Selected Essays*, page 259.

Pericles, the daughter who was lost and is found, for the father the unhoped renewal, and the further promise, of life. Eliot in that poem is under the influence of Shakespeare rather than Dante. It is characteristic and unique; its concern is the defeat of death, the haunting menace, but the only specifically religious or Christian touch in it is the word 'grace'—

> *By this grace dissolved in place.*

It opens:

> *What seas what shores what grey rocks and what*
> *   islands*
> *What water lapping the bow*
> *And scent of pine and the woodthrush singing through*
> *   the fog*
> *What images return*
> *O my daughter*

I don't know where else that note is to be found in the collected poems. My reflection was: surely there is more to be done, in the creative pursuit by Eliot's methods of his kind of spiritual purpose, with human love—with the diverse kinds of human relation covered by that word—than Eliot, with Dante's help, actually does? That, prompted by Harding's remark on the close, is again my reflection when I re-read *Ash-Wednesday*.

Anyone who wants more producible evidence of Eliot's disability, and that it had a significance of the kind I have been suggesting, can find it in *The Cocktail Party*, where it presents itself plainly—in fact, thrusts itself on us. Harding tends to be less severe in adverse or qualifying criticism of Eliot than I am; he notes (the article on the plays is in *Experience Into Words*) that in that play, except for a 'small number of chosen or doomed people, the saints, like Celia, everyone is relegated to the condition of the Chamberlaynes, and the possibility of a deeply satisfying love is excluded without argument'. Harding doesn't draw explicitly the conclusion that seems to me inevitable: Eliot's inner disorder and insecurity, and the lack of self-knowledge that went with them, had grave consequences for him as a spiritual explorer. The plays belong to the social world, where, as I have said, his genius didn't function; their unconscious falsity makes them repellent. The heroic sincerity in which the genius manifested itself belongs to the poetry, giving us there something that is certainly valid. The question is, in what way, within what limits, with what qualifications. It might be suggested, regarding the lack of wholeness of being and fulness of life, that it had, in the poetry, some of the effects of starvation. Among the possible effects of starvation, it might be added, is intensity.

One can't help noticing how the use, for the most intimate purposes, of the *persona* of an old man recurs in the collected poems. You have it as early as *Gerontion* (1920), where the title is confirmed by the opening line:

Here I am, an old man in a dry month . . .

If *Gerontion* is to be described as an imaginative exercise, it remains true that the imagination engaged in it is profoundly engaged; it expresses—it is the servant of— intensely personal preoccupations and moods. The nature of the personal engagement is avowed in the epigraph.

> *Thou hast nor youth nor age*
> *But as it were an after dinner sleep*
> *Dreaming of both.*

That, of course, comes from the Friar's speech to the condemned Claudio in *Measure for Measure*. The theme of the speech is the nothingness of life, and Eliot has picked on the sentence that expresses a sense of the nothingness most poignantly. Such an expression affects us as poignant because of the inner protest that, whether we are conscious of it or not, it evokes in us. And, read as it stands there by itself, the sentence has a sharper effect on readers who remember the context than on others, because of the resonance it carries with it from Claudio's answer: 'Ay, but to die ...' The Friar's speech has been one enforcing the injunction: 'Be absolute for death'. Claudio's answer (for what he says later in the same scene to Isabella is the real and significant answer) is a marvellously potent demonstration that a young man can't be absolute for death. But there is nothing of Claudio in 'Gerontion', and there could hardly be anything more alien to the spirit of his response to the Friar. A response of any kind, of course, is what the poem isn't; for the epigraph is an epigraph, chosen as in resonance with what follows: the suggestion of an ironical dissonance would have had no point. To have recalled and used in that way a disjunct fragment of such a passage, and shown that indifference to so potent a Shakespearian context, seems to me a significant feat. I find it profoundly characteristic.

No one now, I think, will suppose that my attitude towards Eliot is that of a propagandist devotee. It is not, however, merely to protect myself that I have spent so much time making clear the nature of the 'yes, but—'; any more than it was merely with a view to getting my valuation into general currency that I spent a good deal longer appreciating and defining his achievement. I have tried to explain the difficulty my essential purpose puts me in. It commits me to working largely in terms of exemplification, and the necessary exemplifying can be done only by invoking and expressing my own critical judgments. But I am not merely engaged in criticism— my business is not just that of a critical essayist; and my purpose makes it peculiarly important for me to see that you keep well forward in your recognition the fact that I really, consciously and essentially mean the 'isn't it?' that goes with the 'This is so' of a judgment. In giving reasons for suggesting certain lines of study I am necessarily a critic, and I advance my judgments as considered and responsible. But sound as I think them, they close no questions; they are offered as indicating what questions would be involved, what interests and issues presented, what inquiries opened for the student and for those working with him as advisers, collaborators and guides. And this holds of my last critical observa- tions, those I put forward with some insistence by way of eliminating any idea that I want to replace the cult of Yeats with a cult of Eliot.

But there is a more positive way of putting it: though still talking about Eliot I was not the less thinking about Lawrence, and I hoped that my audience would be too. There you have my intention: it was that the relevance of Lawrence, though I didn't name him, should make itself felt, so helping me in the difficult business of suggesting how Lawrence comes in. No one, I hope, expects me to offset my characterization of Eliot's achievement with one of Lawrence's. My undertaking, as I conceive it, doesn't call for that. Nor do I propose to give Lawrence very much direct attention. He doesn't, in relation to my purpose, lend himself to the kind of direct treatment on my part that Eliot invites, and, a not voluminous poet, repays so pregnantly.

But the student, more often than not, can be counted on to have something like a representative acquaintance with the Laurentian *oeuvre*, and to know, in a general way, why in talking about Eliot's peculiar disabilities and limitations I should have been thinking at the same time of Lawrence, and have expected that my audience would be too. Asked why Eliot (quite late) should have testified that, if anyone in our time had stood for the spirit, it was Lawrence and yet, for so long, have been so blind and so rash an enemy of Lawrence's reputation, most students will know, again in a general kind of way, what kinds of issue would be raised in an attempt at answering. A general kind of way is not enough: here—this is the spirit of what I have been saying—are my considered promptings towards the approaches and the lines of inquiry and critical thought that, intelligently pursued, would certainly achieve something closer, more alive and more profitable. No one concerned for humane education at the university would suggest leaving it at that; but I shan't—I needn't, I think—offer any systematic illustration of how a good supervisor, taking or making his opportunities, would, in relation to the given challenge, promote sensitive, energetic and resourceful thinking.

A direct comparison between the poet of *Four Quartets* and the author of *Women in Love* and the tales—I shall certainly not attempt any exemplifying of that. But both were distinguished as critics, and both expressed themselves characteristically in their criticism, and I see some point in suggesting how comparison there brings out the basic contrast they present—brings it out in a way that takes one's thinking back to the creative work.

Both writers expressed themselves critically about *Hamlet*, a work that engaged them profoundly, though, to judge by their accounts of it, it repelled them both. The essay that Eliot wrote with books of Stoll and Robertson in front of him for review is well known. I ought in fairness to say that it doesn't show him at his best as a critic; but then the reason for this is a significant fact about Eliot: he isn't good where criticism involves serious self-committal in value-judgment—that is, he is curiously unsatisfactory where intelligent comment on literature requires a responsive and delicate sense of life. He is at his best in criticism only when the 'practitioner' determines the approach and the focus. One can cap this truth by adding that he shows the firsthand perception and responsiveness of genius in relation to life only in his poetry, his technique (as I have remarked) being a technique for sincerity, and the life being that of which he can cultivate his sense and his knowledge in solitary introspection and meditation. It is notable how in the *Hamlet* essay his distinctive sensibility has a disabling effect on his thought, which ceases to be intelligent, goes in for an illusory (and characteristic) show of trenchancy and precision, and achieves confusion, fallacy and incoherence.

Thus he tells us early in the *Hamlet* essay: '*Qua* work of art, the work of art cannot be interpreted', intending that as a general proposition. If he means that no account of the significance of a work of art can be a substitute for the work itself, that was hardly worth saying. But it is certainly not true that no account of the significance of (say) a Shakespeare tragedy, a James novel, a Lawrence tale or a Blake lyric can have a serious critical function; critical discussion will be largely a collaborative effort to arrive at such an account. Eliot himself is very soon found pronouncing that *Hamlet* 'is most certainly an artistic failure' because—this is his reason—no account of theme or significance that fits the play can be given.

That (he explains) is because Shakespeare has tried to do what can't be done: he has tried to express through Hamlet (the man) 'an emotion which is inexpressible because it is in excess of the facts as they appear'. This conclusion Eliot has prepared for by telling us—a well-known passage: 'The only way of expressing emotion in the form of art is by finding an "objective correlative": in other words, a set of objects, a situation, a chain of events which shall be the formula of that *particular* emotion; such that when the external facts, which must terminate in sensory experience, are given, the emotion is immediately evoked.' The confusion and fallacy here enforce beautifully one of the points I made about Eliot's limitations. The phrase, 'objective correlative', I haven't the least doubt, had served—was serving—a valid use in discussions between Eliot as 'practitioner' and Pound and others, the enemy in view being Georgianism and the use being to insist that poetry isn't talking poetically about and about, but presenting. The misuse here is startling: to identify 'objective correlative' with a 'set of objects', a 'chain of events'—'external facts'—is to reduce significance to what a theatrical producer can under-stand, make the poetry supererogatory, and hand over Shakespeare to the Philistine.

It is true that Eliot in the next sentence illustrates 'exact equivalence' (between 'objective correlative' and 'emotion') by saying: 'you will find that the state of mind of Lady Macbeth walking in her sleep has been com-municated to you by a skilful accumulation of imagined sensory impressions'. But this is a kind of innocent bluff that serves to hinder recognition of the naked crudity. Who actually realizing in what sense a Shakespeare tragedy is *poetic* drama would go on immediately to write: 'The artistic inevitability lies in the complete adequacy of the external to the emotion'—'the external', you see, picking up 'a chain of events' and 'the external facts'? And 'this' (he goes on) 'is precisely what is deficient in *Hamlet*'.

Eliot has already made perfectly plain what spirit of approach this portends, and how drastically it limits the possibilities of 'significance'. 'We find', he says, 'Shakespeare's *Hamlet* not in the action, not in any quotations that we might select, so much as in an unmistakable tone which is unmistakably not in the earlier play'. 'Action' means what a producer would mean by it, and the negative regarding 'selected quotations' doesn't in the least take from the effect of that bland and blank recognition of a mere 'unmistakable tone'. As if 'an unmistakable tone' didn't testify to specific effective and profound significance more impressively than any quotations!

How is this 'tone' (blanket word) conveyed? Not, we gather, by 'objective correlatives'. And there we have the damning comment on Eliot's use of the phrase: it eliminates from all relation to 'significance' the essential poetic function or efficacy of the Shakespearian dramatic poetry. 'Poetic drama is something more than drama in verse'—that, as you know, comes from Eliot himself. It makes a good essay-subject—especially now, in face of the coterie crusade to reimpose Bradley. It comes from the distinguished critic and poet. But Eliot's use of the 'objective correlative' generates confusion, while actually eliminating the orders of significance that make great works of art great. This is the Eliot who, ten years later, and already the author of *Ash-Wednesday* and 'Marina', tells us that 'to have the virtues of good prose is the first and minimum requirement of good poetry'. Hamlet's

emotion is inexpressible because he can't tell us what it is
(nor, behind him, can Shakespeare). That is the position
to which, by dismissing 'tone', Eliot is committed—
except in so far as he saves himself by incoherence and
contradiction. What he *says* is: 'it is inexpressible because
it is in excess of the facts as they appear'. Facts are facts,
and Eliot has made plain what kind of thing 'facts' are.
He adds that it therefore cannot be 'manipulated into
art'—betraying phrase!

Of course, a conception of art (if anything so incoherent
and unaware of what it means can be called a conception)
is implied in all this. Eliot virtually states it when he says:
'The subject' ('the guilt of a mother', he proposes, adding
however a 'but' or 'though') 'might conceivably have
expanded into a tragedy, intelligible, self-complete, in
the sunlight'. The demand that a tragedy, or any creative
work, shall be 'intelligible' in the sense Eliot has sufficiently defined, 'self-complete'—confined like *Coriolanus*
('Shakespeare's most assured artistic success') to a neatly
and comfortably determinate significance, and 'in the
sunlight', so that one can feel there is nothing in it that
one can't clearly and finally see, is arbitrary and vicious.
It reminds one of Lawrence's comment: 'This classiosity
is bunkum; still more, cowardice'. And it makes intelligent appreciation of significant creative works impossible.

What, in short, is involved too is a conception of
intelligence—and an unintelligent one, to which, in his
prose, Eliot is condemned by his own inner disorder,
the nature of which is described by that which he attributes to Hamlet (and Shakespeare). I am not thinking
specifically of the disgust at the 'guilt of a mother', but
of the 'stuff' that the writer (he says) could not 'drag to
light, contemplate, or manipulate into art'—and which

therefore 'remained to poison life'. That way of putting things is not the way of uncompromised intelligence. True intelligence (and this is a most important emphasis for us in our field) is the agent of the whole being, which, of its nature, cannot be brought wholly into the 'sunlight' or 'dragged to light' (a peculiarly betraying infelicity). In *Four Quartets* Eliot does something better than try to 'drag' the inexpressible to light. But a judgment of a limiting kind on the order of creativity *Four Quartets* presents seems to be implied in what I have been saying. I must add at once that creative achievements in which we gratefully recognize a high value can obviously and essentially have been conditioned by limitations and impediments. And even geniuses have to do what they can with what they are.

In talking about Eliot I have again felt myself to be talking about Lawrence too—indeed, primarily about Lawrence. The contrast was always implicit, and the purpose: to evoke the strength that wasn't Eliot's. When, for instance, I spoke of the intelligence that, informed by sensibility, is the agent of the whole being, I knew it was because of Lawrence that I could do that and hope to be understood, and that this would be generally recognized. The given quality of intelligence is beauti- fully illustrated, and with an economy that makes the illustration peculiarly available, in what Lawrence wrote about *Hamlet*. It is to be found in the early book, *Twilight in Italy*, in the chapter called 'The Theatre'.

The Laurentian genius appears in the ease that is an aspect of the economy. It is unmistakably intelligence, and the quick responsiveness of its play suggests a free- flowing fulness of life. It is the great novelist and story- writer who evokes with that spontaneity of vividness the circumstances of the visit to the theatre and the incongruities of the peasant troupe playing *Amleto*, 'una dramma inglese'. The quick sympathetic insight has some amusement in it, but no touch of superiority: the amusement, we feel, while being that, is at the same time, a profound respect for life—for life represented now by humanity making a 'sad fool of itself'. That becomes plain enough to make us say it when the evocation of Enrico Persevalli, carrying a 'long black rag for histrionic purposes', turns (as with an easy felicity it rapidly does) into a criticism of Hamlet himself ('His was the caricature of Hamlet's melancholy self-absorption') and a commentary on the significance of Shakespeare's play. For it doesn't occur to Lawrence to question that the play *has* significance.

It's worth noting that it's not Lawrence, but Eliot who lays the emphasis on sex (and sex gone wrong) in discussing Shakespeare's theme—for that is the effect of making it, so far as any theme is statable, a son's disgust at his mother's guilt. It doesn't occur to Lawrence that anyone might not see the murder of Hamlet, King and Father, as having the importance in relation to the theme of the play that the play itself so strongly insists on. But then it doesn't occur to Lawrence to think the play an artistic failure, or to doubt that it is a significant work. His distinctive contribution to criticism—and that is to thought in general in our field (the non-specialist nature of which let me once more stress)—was a new sense of the kind of thing significance might be, and (at the same time) of the nature of the importance of art to civilization.

For him *Hamlet* is of course the great work the world has taken it to be, though it repels him. It repels him, because he too finds a disgust dominant in it. And for him too the disgust is of such a kind that neither Hamlet nor Shakespeare could explain its significance, nor could the significance be expressed by a 'set of objects', 'a situation', 'a chain of events'—'external facts'. But he would have found the conclusion that it couldn't find expression in Shakespearian poetic drama too absurd to argue about.

The effect of commonsense spontaneity that goes with the quick penetrating perception and the living movement of the thought appears characteristically here:

> I had always felt an aversion from Hamlet: a creeping, unclean thing he seems, whether he is Forbes Robertson or anybody else. His nasty poking and sniffing at his mother, his setting traps for the King, his conceited perversion with Ophelia make him always intolerable. The character is repulsive in its conception, based on self-dislike and a spirit of distintegration.
>
> There is, I think, this strain of cold dislike, or self-dislike, through much of the Renaissance art, and through all the later Shakespeare. In Shakespeare it is a kind of corruption in the flesh and a conscious revolt from this. A sense of corruption in the flesh makes Hamlet frenzied, for he will never admit that it is his own flesh. Leonardo da Vinci is the same, but Leonardo loves the corruption maliciously.

Lawrence relates the plight of Hamlet, and of Shakespeare who created him and transmuted in that disquieting way the traditional Hamlet theme, to a great change in the European psyche. (The last phrase is mine: I have to use my own shorthand.) Hamlet in his 'involuntary soul' (Lawrence's phrase) has decided *not* to *be*—decided that the will to be King, Father and Supreme I (ego) in his turn isn't in him: 'The great religious, philosophic tide, which had been swelling all through the Middle

Ages, had brought him there'. There would be no point in my offering to summarize those fourteen or so astonishing—and to me sufficiently convincing—pages. My purpose is to send you to them, to be considered in the context I have tried to establish.

> The King, the Emperor is killed in the soul of man, the old order of life is over, the tree is dead at the root. So said Shakespeare. It was finally enacted in Cromwell.
> Before Cromwell the idea was 'For the King', because every man saw himself consummated in the King. After Cromwell the idea was 'For the good of my neighbour', or 'For the good of the people', or 'For the good of the whole'. This has been our ruling idea.

There *has* been such a change. And is it obviously absurd to suppose that one finds the crisis of it registered by Shakespeare? I don't think that anyone who has really read and pondered that chapter in Lawrence's book will say so. Question-marks will appear in the margins; some readers will feel more than others that it is not a full or final account of Shakespeare's play; but no one, I think, capable of profiting by the university study of literature will find that it hasn't had a lasting effect on his reading and thinking.

VI
Summing Up: 'Monstrous Unrealism' and the Alternative

SUMMING UP: 'MONSTROUS UNREALISM' AND THE ALTERNATIVE

I DIDN'T adduce Lawrence on *Hamlet* as a model of method of thought, a pattern on which to form one-self. And I don't offer that chapter of *Twilight in Italy* as a satisfying critique of Shakespeare's play. The chapter doesn't offer itself as that—as an essay on the play, concerned to give a balanced account of it. The commentary on Shakespeare is incidental, and any virtue that may be found in it is conditioned by that circumstance. The Italian experiences that Lawrence records in the book are presented in a bent of observation and thought that gives us an insistent preoccupation of Lawrence's. When with that genius of a great novelist he evokes the peasant troupe's *Hamlet*, we aren't led to suppose that the commentary on Shakespeare's play we are given is anything but incidental and partial. The genius that assures us that this commentary comes out of a completer and profounder intelligence about life than Eliot's, and a different sense of the relation between art and life, is there in the vivid, amused, yet sympathetic and un-superior evocation of the incongruities of the scene—the thickset portentousness of Enrico as Hamlet, for instance. And when Lawrence slips with such easy spontaneity into expressing his own 'aversion' from Hamlet we don't suppose that this is offered as a complete critical account of the impression made by the protagonist on a reader of the play. The emphases are not those of criticism. But can we question that Lawrence is calling attention to something commonly ignored in interpretations of the play, and that this something is of great moment? It is something, one can point out, that Wilson Knight emphasizes in two of the essays that made his early—and best—book, *The Wheel of Fire*, an important event in Shakespeare criticism: the two essays on *Hamlet*.

I had better say now (I see) that, if I had a group considering *Hamlet*, the use I should have for Lawrence's chapter would entail the suggestion that they should read it along with a representative set of critiques; say Bradley's, Eliot's, Santayana's, Wilson Knight's and Kitto's. The use of Kitto, the classic who feels himself at home in modern criticism, is monitory; it is that he offers to solve the 'problem of *Hamlet*' by telling us that it is 'religious drama', and lays such a burden of work on the word 'religious' that it does nothing at all. But it is a very important word for the intelligent discussion of Shakespearian tragedy. By way of moving towards a realization of what is meant by saying that, I should prescribe another brief work, Gilbert Murray's British Academy lecture, *Hamlet and Orestes*. Murray there (in 1914—before, that is, Miss Phillpotts' *The Elder Edda* had come out, though, since they must have met, I imagine she and Murray had talked together), taking Hamlet and Orestes as the most popular tragic heroes of the Northern and of classical tradition respectively, brings out the impressive parallel they present, in the main points and in detail. Miss Phillpotts' book (I wonder it is not more used by literary students) establishes that there was a second ritual origin of tragedy in the North, and that a continuity of dramatic tradition runs down through the Middle Ages to Shakespeare,

who, therefore, is at the point of intersection—or junction
—of the two lines.

Now Murray is delicately and very intelligently
suggestive. But the student won't, from reading his
lecture, have learnt how the significance of what he finds
there can be shown to be important for the appreciation
of Shakespearian tragedy—how it can enter into the
understanding of Shakespeare's *Hamlet*. The only help
towards that I know is Lawrence. No one approaching
that chapter in the spirit of my suggestion will be in
danger of taking it anything but critically—but the
finding essential insight in work about which one has to
have critical reserves is a most important order of educational experience. And there *is* insight, decisive prompting
insight, in Lawrence's commentary on *Hamlet*. One may
question the particular formulation he gives of the significance he finds, but the hint and the clue are compelling,
and one realizes that in the tragic Shakespeare—and in
the greatest art—there is significance of that order conveyed: Shakespeare is not only a greater writer than
Racine, but a greater kind of writer.

This last proposition is of course a matter for discussion
—which could be very profitable discussion. As for the
significance of *Hamlet*, Lawrence's account, I said, can
be found decisive and fertilizing by those who question
the particularities of his account. But I'm bound to add
that I don't see why it should be dismissed offhand as
gratuitously Laurentian and obviously absurd. The
murdered elder Hamlet is insistently and potently evoked
as essentially the King, the ideal King and Father—
worthy embodiment of the traditional idea and potency.
No acceptable account of the Shakespearian significance
can ignore that datum. Young Hamlet idolizes his

father, but is presented, surely, as, in the qualities that make him what he is, essentially inconceivable as a second god-like Hamlet. When he proclaims 'It is I, Hamlet the Dane'—this is significant—it is in an aberrant fit of unbalanced bravado for which he later apologizes. And his un-Fortinbras-like complexity is not merely a product of the 'facts' we learn from the play. He has read Montaigne, and is inescapably *of* the post-Mediaeval world. To put it another way, Shakespeare—so intensely alive and receptive in his own time—had read Montaigne (and the student should read J. M. Robertson's *Montaigne and Shakespeare*). Shakespeare, having undertaken to re-write the old *Hamlet*, could with profound imaginative force realize Hamlet the King, but he was also, as we say, a 'modern'—certainly not in the lag of his age. Shakespeare's prince Hamlet didn't—couldn't—'in his involuntary soul' (I use Lawrence's phrase) *want* to be King and Father, supreme I, Hamlet the Dane, the Danish Fortinbras. He couldn't have said that to himself; nor, one supposes, could Shakespeare have said it for him. But who today will suggest that such a significance can't, therefore, be in the play, or that, because the significance can't be brought into the 'sunlight', the play is an artistic failure?

Of course, there is more in *Hamlet*, which is certainly very complex, and in such a way that the difficulty of arriving at an account that satisfies one's total sense of it justifies one's thinking of it as peculiarly a 'problem'. The kind of approach I have been suggesting would certainly not tend more than another to make a student simplify. But it would have brought home to him the force of the judgment that Eliot in his essay is a victim of false assumptions about the nature of significance, and that these involve reductive and anaesthetizing ideas about the nature of great art and the importance of art to civilization.

I won't leave Lawrence's book behind without saying that, outside the chapter called 'The Theatre', it contains a great deal that bears directly on his discussion of *Hamlet*. Particularly in the earlier chapter called 'The Lemon Gardens' there are reflections it would be a pity to miss on the nature and consequences of the profound human change that he sees as the theme of *Hamlet*; and his account of our civilization is the more impressive in that it was written fifty years ago. This quotation must suffice to suggest its relevance to the purpose of these lectures:

> The children are not the future. The living truth is the future. Time and people do not make the future. Retrogression is not the future. Fifty million people growing up purposeless, with no purpose save the attainment of their own individual desires, these are not the future, they are only a disintegration of the past. The future is in living, growing truth, in advancing fulfilment.
>
> But it is no good. Whatever we do, it is within the greater will towards self-destruction and a perfect society, analysis on the one hand, and mechanical construction on the other. This will dominates us as a whole. ... And this great mechanized society, being self-less, is pitiless. It works on mechanically and destroys us, it is our master and our God.

I shall not, I hope, be interpreted as implying that the student (or anyone) will take Lawrence as his authority on the various fields of knowledge, historical and other, these Laurentian commentaries draw on. They assume that the reader has a sufficiency of knowledge to give the reflections their force, and they incite to inquiry, exploration, further acquisition and continued thought. And a reason I will now stress for the attention I have given Lawrence's critique of *Hamlet* is that the thought about history and the nature of our civilization which can be so readily turned to in the book that contains these pages relates intimately to them, and is brought to a focus, and given its sharp edge of meaning, in the interpretation of a great creative work.

We have there, represented with a peculiar force of suggestion, the function of what I will call for convenience the literary-critical intelligence in relation to specialist thought and knowledge. Lawrences are rare, but the example is a potent one. And what it figures and illuminates for us is the liaison function of a university English school, enabling us to realize vividly what it is, and how much it matters. What is the specialist's contribution if it is a contribution only to specialist knowledge and thought? It can have its full human meaning, its *raison d'être*, only in relation to a central human awareness. We can't produce geniuses, but, if we see the need and have the will, we can hope to make the university a humane centre—a centre of intelligence, which here means also full human concern and responsibility.

Well, it's plain by now how little my distribution of my time is an index of the way I expect students to distribute theirs. No one, for instance, will suppose that I don't intend them to give a great deal of attention to the novel. And though I have incidentally (and consciously) established some sort of background and context and bearings for work at the novel, I have said nothing direct and particular to indicate what, I think, should be done and how. Lawrence is a great novelist. Yet few, I imagine, expected that I should play off a representative novel of his against *Four Quartets*. Why didn't I? The

166

answer is plain: the idea is plainly absurd—or is seen to be absurd when it comes to asking how, in the context of a set of half-a-dozen lectures directed to such a purpose as mine, it could be acted upon. And I have been explicit about the way in which I have been using Eliot, and the ways in which he lends himself to it.

Lawrence, as I shall insist, has the stronger traditional roots, and a consideration of them (which I shan't enter into here) amounts to an exposure of Eliot's nonsense (symptomatic, you can call it) about 'tradition'. But Lawrence doesn't lend himself to the illuminating of the present-past relation as Eliot does. The way in which the novel is a new thing—a new *kind* of thing—has a clear relevance to that truth. 'The novel', wrote Lawrence, 'is a great discovery: far greater than Galileo's telescope or somebody else's wireless. The novel is the highest form of human expression so far attained'. The inventing was done in the nineteenth century; the novel in the sense that justifies Lawrence's dictum—makes it, I mean, a serious critical judgment—was created as recently as that, and writers in the English language had a major part in the creating.

The novel, then, can't but be of the first importance for the university study of English literature. The way in which it is new makes it that. Intelligent cultivation of the novel, and thought about it, is likely to have a decisive effect on the conception, the conscious conception and the implicit, of art—of its relation to life and civilization—that informs, not only one's criticism in general, but one's thinking in a wider field. But to recognize the importance is to recognize a problem. To be intelligent about the novel one must have read a good many, and that will entail a great deal of reading of a quality not commonly felt to be called for by novels. Consider how many hours of a student's limited number it will take to read (say) *Little Dorrit* and *Middlemarch* through once. And there will certainly have to be at least one re-reading. But in relation merely to those two works, the attainment of the kind of profit in view entails more than that: the student must know at least something about the respective *oeuvres* to which the works belong, and how can he be intelligent about a given work without a range of reading that gives him a comparative sense of what it is that he has before him? And this last consideration brings me to an aspect of the problem which has a close bearing on the difficulty represented by the limited number of hours in a student's year. I have, as I had to, taken over the classification, 'the novel': what *is* a novel? Can one say more than that the term means a work of fiction of some length in prose?

I came to the conclusion that that was an account generally entertained as sufficient when I listened to a discussion that preceded the instituting of a paper, *The Novel*, in Part II of the English Tripos. And yet once again I was struck by the monstrous unrealism that prevails, at the senior level, in the field of the university study of literature: by the general tacit assumption, or the general lack of any living sense, regarding the amount of reading an undergraduate can be expected to get done, and by the apparent indifference to the considerations that should determine what reading is worth doing. These considerations must relate to a given purpose, and the purpose will be conceived in terms of an intelligent idea of a coherent field of study that can reasonably be prescribed as a subject, or 'paper', the undergraduate having perhaps five others he must qualify himself for in the year—to put it in which way is not to say that I think it reasonable that everything should be staked on end-of-course scribbling against the clock in the examination room.[1] In the discussion to which I have referred the only idea present to the body of participants seemed to be that a novel is a novel and everyone knows what that is. And the preoccupation was the compiling of a list of novels that, together with a specimen set of questions, should give prospective candidates a notion of the way to work for the paper. Unchecked by any less hospitable idea than that I have mentioned, the contributors multiplied and the list grew—Joyce, Proust, Mann, Kafka were added to the English novelists from Richardson (or Defoe) and the Americans and the Russians, and someone pointed out that there was the Elizabethan novel, which led a zealous collaborator to press the claims of *Arcadia*.

To justify a paper you must of course have a subject—or what looks like one; you must in some way limit the field it covers (and it would be better the way should be an intelligent one). But you can't where 'The Novel' is concerned limit the field and make a real subject by definition—definition of what a novel is. To encourage any notion that you *can* is to foster the forms of academicism that are represented by the more sophisticated and crude successors of Percy Lubbock's once well-known book—the treatises on 'the novel', and by the view that Henry James's collected prefaces constitute the 'novelist's *vade-mecum*'.

But I won't—I needn't—say more about that Cambridge project, or the actuality it portended. What I had in mind was to emphasize the immense importance of the

---

[1] The diversity of method—of considerations and tests—by which students of English at York University are classed, deserves to be examined by those who share this doubt.

novel in a literary education that should vindicate the idea
of the university as we must now conceive it; an importance the distinctive nature of which should make a given
kind of study, and a given spirit of frequentation,
obviously the right ones. Our sense that there *is* a subject
derives from the fact that in the nineteenth century a new
development of creative expression, only tardily recognized as belonging to literature, engages the major
geniuses; prose takes over the supreme function of poetic
creation; the modern novel appears. The achievement in
the novel in the English language is one of the great
creative chapters in the human record. In England the
novelists from Dickens to Lawrence form an organic
continuity; the intelligent study of them entails a study
of the changing civilization (ours) of which their work is
the criticism, the interpretation and the history: nothing
rivals it as such.

The unitary field of study for us is there, and the way
of compassing the 'definition' that's needed is to do
enough intelligent work in that field to realize the force
of the recognition. It is essential to exorcise—in the only
way, the positive—the famous image of the timeless
novelists, all writing at a table in one room. Not to do so
would commit the English school to fostering a dis-
astrously enfeebled notion of its distinctive discipline—
criticism, deprive the student of the peculiar approach
to the study of civilization and society that is entailed in
that discipline and make impossible the strong fighting
vindication of university English that we who stand for
the basic human need that the technologico-Benthamite
age denies must offer—must demonstrate—today. For
the bearing of the great tradition of the novel on the
questions with which a rapidly changing civilization con-

fronts us is especially plain, and this is a time when it is desperately necessary to get even the Philistines— especially the Philistines—to see, and acknowledge, some glimpse of significances that don't belong to their world.

I shall be told, possibly, that Lord Snow doesn't matter, and that I have made too much of the representativeness and the evidential value of his way of dismissing the great writers of the industrial age as 'natural Luddites', whose response to the developing new civilization deserves no more attention than that phrase intimates. But the importance of Lord Robbins's attitudes no one can doubt, and Lord Robbins has gone out of his way to prevent our doubting that his, in regard to the kind of effort in education the present state of our society demands, are very much Lord Snow's. In his book, *The University and the Modern World*, we read: 'Since Sir Charles Snow's *Rede Lectures*, we have heard a great deal of the two cultures in this country; for reasons which I completely fail to understand, Sir Charles's very moderate indication of dangers arouses very high passions. To me his diagnosis seems obvious, though it is my experience that the antagonisms he deplores arise chiefly on one side.'

'To me his diagnosis seems obvious'—that seems unequivocal enough: the clichés of the technologico-Benthamite age are clichés of thought—automatisms and blinkers—and they determine the thinking of the able, powerful and influential. And if you believe that there are 'two cultures', whether or not your view of the relation between them is precisely Lord Snow's (and there is no reason for supposing that Lord Robbins's isn't), then you believe that it was a literary person talking nonsense when, in a lecture on Lord Snow's *The Two Cultures*, I myself said, having made some immediately relevant points about the way in which a poem exists for discussion: 'Here we have a diagram of the collaborative process by which the poem comes to be established as something "out there", of common access in what is in some sense a public world. It gives us, too, the nature of the existence of English literature, a living whole that can have its life only in the living present, in the creative response of individuals, who collaboratively renew and perpetuate what they participate in—a cultural community or consciousness. More, it gives us the nature in general of what I have called "the third realm", to which all that makes us human belongs.'

My point was that unless society, responding to the unprecedented conditions of technological civilization— to which we are irrevocably committed, develops by dint of sustained intelligent purpose the habit and the means of fostering in itself this collaborative and creative renewal, the cultural consciousness and the power of response will fade into nullity, and technological development, together with administrative convenience, will *impose* the effective ends and values of life, at the cost of an extreme human impoverishment—as we can see them doing. I have invoked here, briefly and *ad hoc*, the conception I have been trying at some length to communicate of the importance of the literary tradition in our world, and of the essential part of literary study in the idea of a university—in the university the technological age calls for. The nearest Lord Robbins comes to a recognition of any such idea is this: 'To attempt to understand the world, to contemplate and analyse its values—these are activities which, even if they were never associated with practical advantage, would still lend meaning and dignity to life on the planet'. That is the kind of thing that is said in public addresses, and it is not good enough. It merely reveals the frightening unawareness it come out of—unawareness of the kind of menace that closes in on human life.

When Lord Robbins recognizes that, to complement the devotion to the natural sciences, participation in another kind of collaborative effort is required, he gives us this: 'in a complex society such as ours, the hope of order and freedom in social conditions must rest upon the advancement of systematic knowledge in social studies.' And here, he adds, 'as with the natural sciences, the universities have a fundamental contribution to make'. This emphasis on the 'social studies' compels the observation that, unaccompanied by any recognition more adequate than Lord Robbins's of what a university ought to be, it is another disquieting symptom. One begins to recall with some apprehension those admonitory hints one has heard that, to be taken seriously, university English, besides affording a lodgment to linguistic science, must aspire to be a Social Science itself. But the comment immediately called for is that the collective 'social studies', in all their diversity, can't perform the function I have tried to define, and, further, that it would be better for us all if they were pursued and studied, in so far as they aspire to be authoritative sources of knowledge and wisdom about human nature and human life, in the climate, intellectual and spiritual, that a due performance of the function would generate—and in the generating of which an English school would have played, and be playing, an indispensable major part.

As Lord Robbins's attitude exemplifies, we are faced with the extreme difficulty of getting the relevance of literary studies recognized and really believed in. Those who see humane enlightenment itself in his reference to the cardinal necessity of the 'social studies' would no doubt agree very readily that it's a good thing for students of society to know something of Shakespeare, and therefore that Shakespeare studies should be pursued. But this would mean nothing; the readiness with which such a concession is made goes with its conventionality. The novel lends itself much more to a demonstration of relevance—the relevance (I mean, in the first place) of a study in that field to academic concerns that Lord Robbins recognizes as important; and the advantage is at the same time one to be made the most of within the school itself. One can point out, with an eye on the great English line, that the novelists are incomparable students and critics of society and civilization, and incomparable social historians. A senior intelligently interested can direct (with profit to himself) a manageable study that will, for the student, enforce the truth and bearing of that observation. Such a study, while serving the liaison function ideally, would, where the menace with which the modern world confronts us is in question, bring out the way in which the distinctive intelligence of the major novelist is essential and irreplaceable.

I can best explain with brevity what I mean in terms of Dickens. And that will enable me to do at the same time something that badly needs doing, which is to make an indignant protest against the established attitude to that very great writer. The world of academic literary studies, so far from offering to vindicate Dickens's genius, steadily endorses and confirms the attitude in its own practice; and the literary world could plead that scholars and Dickens specialists provide the prompting and the authority. Dickens is of course a genius, but 'as soon as he begins to think he is a child': there you have the attitude. That last definitive phrase, I remember, clinched a formula in which, some years ago, two distinguished academic collaborators assured the public of embarrassing disability as accepted and unquestioned fact. Quite recently a contributor to a book of essays on Dickens dismissed the view that the Horse-Riding in *Hard Times* plays a clear and important part in a total anti-Benthamite significance with an appeal to the truism that Dickens, though of course (we all know) a genius, is merely an entertainer, so that to find subtle significances in a book of his is obviously absurd. A Horse-Riding is a circus, and a circus is entertainment, and the significance of the chapter (it's called 'The Loophole') is simply: 'All work and no play makes Jack a dull boy.' Moreover, Dickens wasn't capable of understanding Bentham.

Then there is Professor Philip Collins, a well-known Dickens specialist. In the last book of his I read, *Dickens and Education*, he again makes it plain that he doesn't see how the attitude can be seriously challenged. This is a characteristic passage: 'To the vivid concreteness and the vast profusion of detail in his writing one may relate his enjoyment for seeing and reading about things and activities, rather than contemplating ideas and abstractions. (There are, alas, passages of generalization in the novels, the embarrassing banality of which corresponds all too faithfully to this gap in his intellectual equipment.)' Professor Collins plainly feels—and there is nothing in the book to qualify the conclusion—that he has closed here all possibilities by which Dickens might escape the charge of 'intellectual banality' (inability to think—he was 'lacking in intellectual vigour').

The failure to notice the magnificent intelligence in

which Dickens's genius manifests itself is a failure to notice that he is a great artist, the notion of art and the notion of intelligence—an inadequate one can do the mischief—being involved together. That is made beautifully plain in a sentence like this: 'Another such device is his describing the hopeless childhood of some of the criminal characters, such as Nancy in *Oliver Twist* and Magwitch in *Great Expectations*, with which he wishes us to sympathize'. That—I put it in this way in order to insist relevantly on the force of an important word—is very emphatically not an intelligent observation. Nancy and Magwitch are both criminals and both presented as victims of society, it is true; but Nancy comes from an early and immature work, while Magwitch belongs to one of the great European novels, of which he, in his essential relation with Pip, forms a major part of the theme.

Great Expectations is an intensely 'engaged' study (I mean, it is at the other extreme from the abstract, statistical and theoretical) of society, done in terms of individual lives, one of which is presented with a sustained and searching inwardness. It implicitly says 'This is your England', and the claim is sufficiently substantiated, the intention sufficiently achieved, to make the book profoundly impressive as what it offers to be, and—one ought to be able to say—of great importance as such to those who are studying society, human nature and human possibilities now, a hundred years later. It is so truly and vitally intelligent, in a great novelist's way, about human beings and the society they are formed by and form, that its significance is missed by those who write studies of Dickens as a social critic, and even by those who write in the Sunday magazine pages—so that I may perhaps permit myself to remark that to call Pip a snob and *Great Expectations* a 'Snob's Progress' is not only unintelligent, but indecent—unless one said it in inverted commas as coming from Pip himself.

But I am not embarking on a critique of Dickens. Merely, there is a certain minimum I have to say by way of enforcing my theme. And to come back to *Hard Times*: the undergraduate—or the senior—who has taken the significance of the book, and recognized the finality with which it leaves the Benthamite calculus, the statistical or Blue Book approach, and the utilitarian ethos placed, can say why neither a 'rising standard of living', nor equality, nor both together, will do when accepted as defining the sufficient preoccupations and aims of thought and effort, and why to be able to posit *two* cultures is a dangerous form of unintelligence. It is in *Hard Times* that the relation to Blake asserts itself and is (to me, at any rate) unmistakable. But the little I can allow myself to say about it had better be said in connexion with the later and supremely great major work, *Little Dorrit*.

Little Dorrit is an inquest into civilization in the mature Dickens's contemporary England. What Professor Collins makes of it as a work of art—makes, that is, of a supreme demonstration of the intelligence we are so badly in need of—is presumably intimated here: 'like his novels, his History [of England] deals with vivid characters, seen externally, engaged in dramatic and generally reprehensible action, shown in a macabre or ludicrous light'. Yet in fact everything in *Little Dorrit*, including the 'melodramatic' *dénouement* is significant, to say which is to say that, for all the abundance and range, the organization is strong and vital. And the significance

177

regards the meaning of life, and entails an exploration of human experience and a critique of human satisfactions and ends.

One asks, as one reads and ponders: what are the things, the qualities, the human manifestations that Dickens positively values, and in relation to which he orders his criticism of Victorian life and society—finds himself ordering it as he feels his way into the organization of his novel? and how are they related to one another? The deep affinity with Blake comes out in the answers. I remember noting down, as the text prompted me with them, the words that registered the answers that took form. The words, of course, in themselves do little: they point to the charged and definitive significances that the novel, the dramatic poem, creates and conveys. The words I set down are 'disinterestedness', 'love', 'spontaneity', 'energy', 'creativeness', 'art'. I will resist the temptation to comment on them beyond saying once again that for Dickens as for Blake there is a continuity from the creativeness of perception (I represent by that the elementary manifestations of life) to the developed and disciplined creativeness of the artist, in whom spontaneity goes with trained skill, and that the genuine representative of art in *Little Dorrit* is Daniel Doyce, the inventor—as opposed to the bogus artist, Henry Gowan, who *hasn't* disinterestedness, energy or love (he *has* instead plenty of ego).

I hope I have said enough to give force to my insistence that in Dickens's art a potent social criticism, for which lives can't be averaged, conflated or aggregated, involves the invocation of values that can't be stated abstractly or numerically, or reduced to quantity. Of course, Dickens also went in for the kind of 'social criticism' that the writers of the books are thinking of when they use that formula to define their subjects, and that fact counts a great deal in his importance from my present point of view. The student is properly required to have a know-ledge, not only of the indebtedness to Carlyle (and so of Carlyle's significance), but of the influence on Dickens of the thought and climate in general, and the social and political history, of his time. For though it is beside the point to demonstrate that he had no practical wisdom to offer as to how reforms were to be effected, and no coherent political philosophy, it doesn't follow that his reformer's preoccupations had no significant bearing on that social criticism of his which can't be relegated— that is, the essential. The distinctive genius in him fed on his experience, and in this the reformer's impulse and effort played a great part; without them his insight and the creation it informed wouldn't have been what they were.

And I am certainly not suggesting that it would be a good thing if the student went into the world believing that Benthams, practical reformers and statesmen could well be dispensed with. The influential public that it seems to me so urgently important to produce wouldn't favour that line. Its function would be to keep reforming political and administrative activity from blindness and indifference to any but short-term ends. And an essential qualification for that role is the wisdom that goes with an awareness of complexities.

I won't make any show of suggesting how much towards becoming intelligent about the novel from Dickens to Lawrence the student could be counted on to get done. My business is to emphasize the difference between the right kind of partialness, patchiness and in-completion and what is favoured by those who dismiss as 'provincial' the spirit I have tried to define. Better, then, be provincial than cosmopolitan, for to be cosmopolitan in these matters is to be at home nowhere, and he who is at home nowhere can make little of *any* literature—the more he knows, the larger is his ignorance. The student who has worked, and been guided, on the lines and in the spirit I have been describing has in him, if he is fitted for advanced literary study at all, the principle of organic growth, and can make something real of his opportunities in regard to foreign literatures. And he will have the perception and the means of judgment that will enable him to protect himself—to see, for example, the absurdity (and the portent) of being offered a Hemingway as a great or profoundly interesting writer, or a Scott Fitzgerald as a talent who calls for earnest study.

I interpolated 'portent' because the American influence in university English continues to grow, and it is a bad one, which, for America's sake as well as our own, we should resist. There is a great deal to be said for having a study, extended to form an approach to Mark Twain and James, of what Lawrence called 'classic American literature'. That, intelligently directed, would bring, besides (in the narrower suggestion of 'literary') the diverse literary gains, a knowledge of that divergence in civilization the upshot of which, so largely a matter of reconvergence, concerns us so momentously to-day, being for us so pregnant with significance. But to ask undergraduates to devote a proportion of their in any case insufficient time to a set study of 'modern American literature' is another thing. It means expecting them to acquire facility in retailing the pseudo-criticism that treats as classics and masters an array of writers for treating whom in that way, or any approaching it, no good reason can be found. What's in question is worse than a waste of time.

But it's the more general menace that I have in mind. It is an American ethos that prescribes these cosmopolitan cures for our provinciality, and the idea that being provincial is what we suffer from is itself American. I ought to add at once that the intrinsic movement of civilization in this country has in any case been taking us towards an American consummation, so that actual American influence finds a ready and profound response. That comes out revealingly in one of those gratuitous remarks which, addressing his audiences, Lord Robbins from time to time finds consonant with his purpose: 'We all', he told one of them, 'know the type—the sort of person who gets hot under the collar when he thinks of Lord Snow's Rede Lecture, the sort of person who looks down his nose when you mention American universities'. The assumptions, the bent and the temper are plain: suggest that American experience in the field of education provides us with anything other than a model, and you are placed—placed outside all serious discussion. The Americans I have talked with don't take that line. Not only have they all been ready to point out with great particularity that very different kinds of thing share the description 'university' in the United States, but one I spoke with recently said, in regard to present British educational policy generally—having probed, and found that it *could* be said to me: 'It's strange: you in this country are plunging deliberately into the same mistakes that *we* made, and from the consequences of which *we* are now struggling to escape.'

I will say, then, that the prescription of wide-ranging

cosmopolitanism belongs, like the diagnosis 'provincial', to the ethos of a world for which, the phrase having been once thrown out and publicized, there are obviously *two* cultures, and it's nonsense to urge that the problem is one of preserving, while it is still a living continuity, the only one we have—to keep it alive and in growth. But it's very far from being nonsense, and no one who realized how much other than nonsense it is would prescribe a 'great books', or 'great authors', syllabus, or anything tending towards it, or the mixed courses that are being established so generally in our new universities. It is a vital necessity that something real in humane education, involving a central and genuine discipline of intelligence and the acquiring of an inward knowledge of English literature, should be done at university level somewhere. It will certainly not be done where there are those acclaimed 'new break-throughs', the upshot of which, where it isn't discouragement and despair, will be sciolism and bogus intellectuality.

Of course, the kind of study I have been defining as proper to a university implies that the students will be truly of university standard. But this country has become Americanized in the sense that it has taken over, or developed for itself, the American conception of democracy. In neither country will it be allowed to prejudice at all seriously our technological advance and it has no tendency at all to discourage athletic distinction— natural inequality there is recognized, fostered and exploited. But in the matters of our present concern there is nothing to check the democratic principle, according to which anything in the nature of an intellectual *élite* is to be jealously guarded against—nothing except the conviction of those who know what is at stake. If we know and care, then we must tell ourselves that we have, and shall have continually, to fight. That is our responsibility towards society, which doesn't know what its malady is.

That it *has* a malady it is very much aware: everyone has heard of that lack of a 'sense of purpose'. I read on that theme last year in the *Spectator*—where I also read that the achievement of the World Cup made one proud to be British—an article, or address (which the Editor thought important enough to reprint), by Lord Radcliffe: 'The Dissolving Society', it was called (May 13, 1966). The spirit of my remarks isn't one of adverse criticism; I am invoking an illustration that seems to me very much to the point. Lord Radcliffe is a distinguished man who has had much opportunity to observe, and about his seriousness there could be no doubt. He listed many signs of the malady, and he dismissed, rightly I think, the suggestion that loss of the empire or loss of power explained the loss of a 'sense of purpose'. But when he came to his last paragraph, and felt the need to end with something positive, all he could say was: 'We must, I think, get back quickly to the active realization of our identity as a nation'.

I have no intention of disrespect when I say that that seems to me a frightening confession of hopelessness. Not that I have any answer to the problem Lord Radcliffe was, in his own way, calling attention to. There is, in the nature of things, no answer to be given, and nothing simple can helpfully be said. But that doesn't mean that society, through the proper organ, cannot and should not be making an effort of a kind that is beyond any serious question relevant. The proper—the only proposable—organ is the university.

Rapid and immense change is in front of us. Who can foresee what relation, in a few decades' time, the maintenance of a cultural tradition—our own cultural tradition —will bear to the nation-state as we know it?—for in his phrase about a 'sense of national identity' it is the nation-state as we know it that Lord Radcliffe seems to be assuming. Mankind is certainly going to develop new kinds and modes of organization. Our business, our vital need, is to maintain the continuity of life and consciousness that a cultural tradition is, and not to lose anything essential from our heritage—the heritage that is only kept alive by creative renewal (which means change) in every present. If we contrive to have an influential educated public, a responsible public that cares for and represents the heritage and is concerned (as such a public will be) to get it shared as widely as possible, we shall hear much less of the lost sense of purpose. And we can't foresee what, by its creative action in the third realm (which the technologico-Benthamite world despises and ignores) a living cultural tradition may do for humanity.

In any case, I don't believe that America, for all its wealth and power and its prospect of getting first to the moon, or even its athletic pre-eminence, has more of a 'sense of purpose' than this country has, or is in a more satisfying spiritual—or human—state. The assumption to the contrary is a characteristic illusion, or symptom, of the civilization we live in.

APPENDICES

Of the three items I print below under this head, the last—and longest—is the one that answers obviously to the ordinary suggestion of the word 'appendix'. The theme of 'Research in English' has clearly a very important relevance to the preoccupation of my lectures, but the enforced economy of the course left no time to deal with it.

I reproduce and print first my letter to *The Times* by way of reminding the reader how brutally political, practical and menacing the realities are that present themselves as enlightenment and dedicated zeal for that basic matter: reform in the field of education.

The second appendix is a pregnant note on 'vacuity' (see page 24 above) which should help to give force to that word, bringing home to us how rapid has been the process of change and how subtly the most essential deprivations have gone along with it. Rilke wrote it in 1925. We should not today think of the 'empty, indifferent things' as 'crowding over from America'; they are so much a product of the industrial civilization that belongs natively here, in Great Britain and Europe, and to which we belong.

APPENDIX I

THE FUNCTION OF THE UNIVERSITY

The following letter appeared in *The Times* of January 22, 1968:

Sir,—Lord Annan, in his letter (January 19), exhibits, as stern admonisher, the strength and the courage of representativeness: the world, he knows, is with him. The menace with which he backs his injunction to the universities is not an idle one. In fact, there is no more urgent duty soliciting those who are concerned for the real interests of the community than to resist the blind forces Lord Annan so confidently points to.

N   185

Of course, we all know that desperate crises may call for desperate measures—for recourses that wouldn't seem capable of defence unless we told ourselves they were very strictly ad hoc and exceptional. But Lord Annan, while invoking the immediate crisis, makes it plain that the step he prescribes is to be a commitment to a permanent surrender—surrender of something he identifies with 'privilege'.

The universities, he says, 'could offer to lay on residential courses of a month's length in the summer for children who would have stayed on at school but for the postponement. . . .' Reassuring us with the datum that the 'drop-out rate among such teen-age students is very high', he tells us: 'A month's intensive teaching might work wonders and enable more to qualify'—i.e., to pass examinations. But why, one asks, should university teachers be supposed to be qualified for that kind of cramming, which is utterly at odds with the qualifications that, as university teachers, they have in long experience acquired, and by reading, thought, pondered experience and hard work continually renew and bring up to date?

Lord Annan, with the menace-enforced 'must' of the following, provides the answer: 'If the universities are not to be attacked as citadels of privilege, they must give what help they can.' We are to understand that, in the near future, there will be the closest relation between a university teacher's qualifications and those needed for the emergency; helping let-down teen-agers to 'qualify' in spite of their having not been prevented from leaving school at 15—coaching them for their examinations—will be immediately relevant training: 'When the sixth form curriculum is reformed, they [the universities] will have to provide more elementary teaching for their own students, and it would be useful to get experience in providing it.'

The 'privilege' the universities must surrender lest they be attacked as anti-democratic citadels is the right (or duty) to maintain the standards proper to a university. Of course 'university' now, in this country, too, is a term applied to some very different kinds of thing—there is, for instance, the Open University, there are correspondence colleges that hope to become universities, and Mr Wilson not long ago expressed his satisfaction that a number of Colleges of Technology had swelled the total of universities (a snub for snobbery, he thought).

Lord Annan's letter (he is still a Provost) exemplifies the dangers associated with this liberal use of the term. Essential truths have been almost forgotten. Firstly, the phrase 'the standards proper for a university' means something. Secondly, to identify the problem of Higher Education with the idea of the university is disastrous; for, thirdly, if standards are not maintained at the university the advance of Higher Education will (for one thing) be grievously disabled.

Neither democratic zeal nor egalitarian jealousies should be permitted to dismiss or discredit the fact that only a limited proportion of any young adult age group is capable of profiting by, or enjoying, university education. The proper standards can be maintained only if the students the university is required to deal with are—for the most part, at any rate—of university quality. If standards are not maintained somewhere the whole community is let down.

Your faithfully,
F. R. LEAVIS

APENDIX II
RILKE ON VACUITY

The following extract from the letter sent by Rainer Maria Rilke to his Polish translator in 1925 is quoted (as translated) by J. B. Leishman in the Introduction to his text-and-translation edition of *Sonnets to Orpheus* (Hogarth Press), page 19:

> ... the ever swifter vanishing of so much that is visible, whose place will not be supplied. Even for our grandparents a 'House', a 'Well', a familiar tower, their very dress, their cloak, was infinitely more, infinitely more intimate; almost everywhere a vessel in which they found and stored humanity. Now there come crowding over from America empty, in-different things, pseudo-things, dummy-life. ... A house, in the American sense, an American apple or wine, has nothing in common with the house, the fruit, the grape into which the hope and pensiveness of our forefathers would enter. ... The animated, experienced things that share our lives are coming to an end and cannot be replaced. We are perhaps the last to have still known such things. On us rests the responsibility of preserving not merely their memory (that would be little and unreliable), but their human and Laral worth ('Laral' in the sense of household-gods).

In the same Introduction Leishman refers to the passage from the tenth of the Duino Elegies about the City of Pain by which we are reminded of the significant way in which, in America, the intensified spiritual Philistinism of our civilization is associated with assiduous evasion of the fact of death:

> Oh aber gleich darüber hinaus,
> hinter der letzten Planke, beklebt mit Plakaten des 'Todlos',
> jenes bitteren Biers, das den Trinkenden süss scheint,
> wenn sie immer dazu frische Zerstreuungen kaun . . .,
> gleich in Rücken der Planke, gleich dahinter, ists wirklich.
> Kinder spielen, und Liebende halten einander,—abseits,
> ernst, im ärmlichen Gras, und Hunde haben Natur.

APPENDIX III
RESEARCH IN ENGLISH

I read in *The Times Literary Supplement* for 28 June the leading article entitled 'Tangible Results' and felt a strong impulse to write and express my gratitude. When I started to act on the impulse I soon found myself in difficulties. Correspondence printed in the succeeding issue confirmed both my sense that the opportunity I had seen the article as presenting ought to be taken and my realization that the taking would not be such a simple matter of direct comment as would lend itself to the necessary brevity of a letter.

'Perhaps the time is ripe for some research into the nature of literary research': when I read this closing suggestion of the letter printed from Mr Philip Hobsbaum I was moved to something that might be called assent. But I saw that he didn't really share the conviction that had been troubling me, a strong sense of the grounds for which (and of the urgent need to get recognition for them) being my own response to the article in *The Times Literary Supplement*: the conviction that it is high time for some thinking about the nature of 'research' as it should be understood in university English Schools. I intimate in this last clause my view that the right answers to the questions that need to be asked will hardly be arrived at unless the inquiry into the nature of 'literary research' subserves—and is thought of as subserving—a concern for an adequate conception of liberal education and the university.

What made it clear to me that Mr Hobsbaum didn't share at any rate the intensity of my conviction was his general optimism. The review accompanying the leading article and providing its occasion had dealt with some depressingly futile products of the American academic industry. Referring to it, Mr Hobsbaum remarked that the 'reviewer . . . was probably attacking something already dead'. 'That is too easily said' gives my reaction to that comment. I mean, there *is* a menacing academicism against which we have to be militantly upon our guard—a form of academicism institutionally established and invincible in America, and one the tendency towards which in this country—the developments of civilization favouring it—is much strengthened by American influence (so many of our politically dominant academics and our 'coming' younger ones have spent some time at American universities). The apprehension I express—and I know I am not alone in feeling it—is not to be dismissed by the reminder that there have been good books written as theses for the Cambridge Ph.D., or the assurance that we are unlikely to have a proliferation of the blankly or brutally crass kinds of doctoral manufacture here.

Whatever there may be to be said about the reminder or the assurance, I myself have, for the past dozen years or so, watched a pertinacious drive to establish in Cambridge 'English' what I may properly call the American idea of research and its place in university education. Such a drive—a drive (one to be feared and fought) for such an end—could hardly in those early days of the Ph.D., forty-odd years ago, when the English Tripos was finding and asserting its distinctive character, have been thought of as possible. No one supposed that research in relation to the English School could be anything analogous in status and essential importance to what it was in relation to the scientific departments.

The Ph.D., we gathered, has been instituted with an eye to the expectations of young American graduates who might be expected in the future to contemplate coming to England instead, of going to Germany. By a kind of accident (it seemed—for Balfour or whoever had promoted the idea, would hardly have thought of the critical study of English literature, to which we were committed as a relevant academic field), we too, we of the English Tripos, had the benefit of this new institution, Ph.D. research. And we quickly established an implicit understanding of the way in which it could be made truly a benefit; in ten or a dozen years we had established the appropriate tradition. (I say 'we', a suitably indeterminate word, suggesting as it does the unofficial, informal and non-authoritative: the thing was not done by way of committees, reports, boards or re-formulated regulations.) 'Research' in English was seen as providing opportunities for men and women who had distinguished themselves in the English Tripos to go on with their education and the discovery of their interests and powers,

learn how to carry through a sustained piece of constructive thinking in the exploration of some congenial theme or field, and, in
short, to improve their qualifications for discussing literature with
intelligent undergraduates—helping them to conduct their
studies profitably and to make the most of their opportunities.

This was the simple direct account to be given, we thought, of
'research' in English—the short answer to the question, how was
its place in the scheme of things to be thought of. But of course a
comprehensive account would have entailed a good deal more, and
raised a certain complexity of considerations. When, by way of
intimating what these were, I invoke *Scrutiny*, I bring out the
force of my 'we'. There are two statements to be made with
immediate point: (i) *Fiction and the Reading Public*, which was
written as a doctoral thesis in the English School, was a major
relevant fact behind the founding of *Scrutiny*; (ii) *Scrutiny* emerged
out of the informal gatherings ('social'—in the pursuit of their
intellectual interests) of a number of research students round a
friendly hearth.

If there had not been the English Tripos, with the consequent
notion of 'research' that represents its ethos at the level of post-
graduate studies, there would have been no *Scrutiny*. The *Scrutiny*
group, in fact, in the days when the new enterprise was being
engendered and founded, had much to do with the establishing of
the distinctive Cambridge tradition of 'research' in English—as
even a relaxed turning-over of the volumes will make pretty clear.
A number of those who frequented the milieu has subjects that
may fairly be said to have been inspired by *Fiction and the Reading
Public*. In fact, had not authority at the centre of power in the
English School detected an illicit influence and, resolving that this
kind of thing must not be allowed to go on, made its will to be discouraging very plain, Cambridge would before the war have
unmistakably had a 'school', if an unofficial one, of what is nowa-
days conveniently referred to as 'literary sociology'.

I am not meaning to suggest that we thought of all 'research'
as being of that kind; very much the contrary. The stress fell on
'literature' and 'criticism': our concern was for kinds of study in
which, though they might not perhaps be classifiable under literary
criticism, the part of the literary-critical intelligence should be

essential and fundamental. And such study, much stimulated and nourished by *Scrutiny* (for all the official non-existence of that offending insistence of life) went on at Cambridge. Its product, direct and indirect, is to be seen on a large scale in the volumes of *Scrutiny*.

I refer to *Scrutiny* in this way because to do so is essential to the key point I have to make. It is agreed, I hope, that, as Mr Hobsbaum suggested, there has been a need for some thinking about the nature of 'research' in English. It is plain, for instance, that, for our purposes, the phrase 'a genuine contribution to knowledge' has a marked infelicity, and that research in relation to an English School can have no close analogy with research in the sciences. On the other hand, 'research' properly conceived (there is a convenience in retaining the term) has nevertheless an essential part of play if the English School is to be that which it should be: that which, generating in the university a 'centre of human consciousness—perception, knowledge, judgment and responsibility', should make it really a university; that is, more than a collocation of specialist departments. 'It is assumed', I said in my Richmond lecture, *Two Cultures?* (for the sake of economy, I will permit myself a further brief quotation—the context can be examined by anyone interested enough),

'that work in the scientific departments must be in close touch with the experimental-creative front. In the same way, for the university English School there is a creative front with which, in its function and nature, the School must be in the closest relation. I am not thinking of the fashionable idea that the right qualification for a teaching post is to be a poet—or a commercially successful novelist. I am thinking of what *Scrutiny* stood—and stands—for: of the creative work it did on the contemporary intellectual cultural frontier in maintaining the critical function.'

The point that I am insisting on is that the governing conception of 'research' we need in English will not be arrived at by trying to find some suitable formula that will serve better than 'genuine contribution to knowledge' to describe the good thesis. There are clearly a number of acceptable kinds. Research has to be thought of in relation to the whole 'idea' of the university English School. The representative research student (there is a good deal of point in thinking in terms of *him*—or *her*) should be a person of some distinction of mind and exceptional enterprise and self-reliance, capable of proposing for himself a sustained piece of work worth doing and of carrying it through, whose presence in the community clearly tends to strengthen it as the milieu of creative inter-course it ought to be.

For it is only in terms of maintaining and strengthening the life of such a community that the educational problem itself—the university's problem of humane education—can be seriously thought about without something like despair. Of course, to have an intelligently conceived syllabus or field of study, free from wasteful or frustrating requirements, for the student—that matters to him directly in the most obvious way. It matters to him also, and not less, by way of its mattering so much to his teachers and guides, and it matters to them in making it possible for mature minds capable of first-hand judgment and creative thought to pur-sue the development of their interests on the frontiers while at the same time (the better teachers for it) drawing stimulus from their 'teaching' and from their contacts in general with undergraduates— representatives of lively, expectant and disinterested intelligence.

It is partly the role of research students to be among those senior members of the community, and, in close touch as they are with the younger world, they have an essential liaison function. It matters to them, too, and in the same way (with advantage again at the undergraduate level) that there should be intelligent teaching for them to do. They are, in fact, a necessary element in the total community that 'English' in a university ought to be—must be, if 'English' is to perform its function as central humanity, and count at all significantly in relation to the sciences: the community that makes it possible for the undergraduate member to get the higher education that cannot, when we inquire into its nature and possibilities, be adequately suggested in terms merely of syllabus and kinds of instruction. My stress falls generally on the collaborative total interplay that constitutes the 'community' and particularly on the necessary part in it of the research student (the right kind of research student), if work in the English School is to answer seriously to an account of it as 'in touch with the creative front'.

There is a battle to be fought everywhere, and, as I have said, in this matter of research it clearly has to be fought at Cambridge. The living actual tradition of research from which Cambridge 'English' benefited so much was tacit and informal. The drive I refer to is calculated, concerted and pertinacious and aims at new official and institutional provision—amounting, in fact, to the establishing of something in the nature of the American Graduate School. Its promoters have a habit (and one's pointing out that there is no valid comparison does not seem to trouble them) of producing statistics to show how much greater is the percentage of research students at American universities than at Cambridge. But the argument starts on a humane note—a note of compassionate concern for the hordes of depressed research students who have been admitted to research in English, but just cannot get on, and need *much* more help. I have found that all the intelligent research students I meet recoil from the idea of having to have such help and evade the campaigning and self-proffering helpers as much as they dare.

The scale on which research students are to be assumed in future to need help is intimated in the proposal that a University Lecturer who carries the burden of 'looking after' half a dozen research students should be let off one of the courses of lectures for which he is salaried. One's comment is that a graduate who needs that amount of help should never have been admitted as a research student. Positively, one invokes the hitherto unquestioned criterion: the type research student should be the First Class Tripos man, judged to be capable of sustained independence and self-direction, and needing in the matter of help only a standing relation with a congenial senior to whom he can go now and then for criticism and advice. The reply one gets is a polite bow to the superannuated ideal, and a recall to realism. The university has a new duty, we are told: there is a besieging host, ever-increasing, of Indians, Africans, Commonwealth people in general, Levantines, who aspire to become university teachers of English literature, and must therefore have a Ph.D.—preferably a Cambridge one (though it is admitted that a large proportion of them couldn't hope to take the English Tripos with much credit—even if they could pass).

In this reply the significance of the drive is plainly avowed. And the rejoinder is clear and unanswerable: no alleged new duty can abrogate the duty of Cambridge to maintain the standard. No one questions that in respect of the sciences, and it holds no less of 'English'. Of course, in 'English' the problems of defining the nature of standards, getting recognition for them, and ensuring enforcement are harder. And that makes the burden of responsibility resting on Cambridge the heavier—for reasons of history, which have given Cambridge some advantages, so that it is reasonable to fear that if the standard is not maintained there it won't be anywhere. I am thinking of the inimical pressures which are everywhere insistent and insidious.

To debase 'research' in the way proposed is not merely to deprive the 'community' of which I have spoken of an essential element of life. Those concerned for the English School at any university should recognize clearly that if they permit anything of the kind there will be general disastrous concomitants, and that the corruption entailed in conniving (and more than conniving) at the sending out as highly qualified university teachers people who are very far from being that, and often grossly unfit—sending them out with a hallmark to which they have no right—will have a general corrupting influence. They should stand firm on the principle that a research student should be a distinguished mind, with exceptional enterprise and self-reliance, and that the mark of the genuine research student is that he has something he wants to do. But the specialized director of research, with his card-index from which he is ready to hand out subjects—*he* will certainly come with the kind of regime proposed, and he will be a centre of blight. For he will remain in the English School, he will be felt in the prevailing ethos, he will still be a university teacher, and he will examine as well as instruct undergraduates.

Whatever is to be done for the sub-standard would-be researcher, towards whom it is felt we have a duty, there must be a resolute and uncompromising concern to ensure that standards are in no way prejudiced and the rights of the genuine research student are not touched. That will be difficult, but it is surely plain that any solution by compromise will be stultifying.

The desperate need today is that 'English' should justify the claim it is committed to making: that it provides something real and irreplaceable, a discipline unequivocally genuine and deserving the respect of scientists.

This material was first published in *The Times Literary Supplement* and subsequently in *The Critical Moment* (Faber & Faber 1964). Thanks are due to Times Newspapers Ltd. and to Faber & Faber Ltd. for kind permission to reprint it here.